i. (kairos)

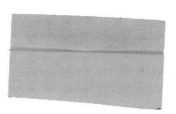

III

when she's busied with the sensible

~~██████████~~

AND   ~~████~~ against ~~████████~~

~~████████~~ by the figure ~~██████████~~

~~███~~ no one has to cut their hair,

as a sign of mourning for the ~~████████~~

~~█~~ rhythmic enclave

> me yes him
>
> you yes him
>
> him yes him

~~███████~~ in separation from the ~~██████~~

~~████~~ the third kind

~~████████~~ articulated ~~██████~~

~~██████████~~ fate

dispensing with assertion causes ~~████████████~~

mediation of ~~██████████████~~

a month's worth of notebook writings ~~██████████~~

~~████████████~~ at Canessa

~~██████████████████~~ be the right kind of

~~██████~~ y self like they said soul?

to keep desire alive

EV   ✍ diapheron heauto

aoristic ~~████████████~~,

~~████████~~ debt to ~~██████~~

~~███~~ destitution of the ~~████████~~

future contingents

ground ~~susidence~~ subsidence & structural damage

"in actually almost going through with it, we found a distinction"

"i'll swallow just to feel your hand feeling ~~██~~

~~████████████~~ this ~~██████████~~

~~████████~~ distance from those objects which seduce us into thinking we ourselves are them

all is ~~this~~ ~~port of~~
for bad debt.

all is ~~this~~ full of labor,
the tongue cannot utter it

~~it rests by changing~~

labor, univocal in the human world

~~the ~~ another name for

~~our~~ boundless vows

~~good friends~~, affliction is ~~enlightenment~~

~~to be free~~ of form amid ~~forms~~
the
~~this fills~~ gap twixt text & the ~~world~~

~~out~~ machine translation of
ta onta

where all elements
translatable
are
~~enlightenment is~~ also a kind of forgetting

cash catachresis

ducats is the monad
into which all folded
sleep the sleep of the debt

of just price

that spans ~~the~~ expanse of forms

of military grain,
~~the~~ laid up,
~~immutable~~ of
~~noble metal~~,
not to oxidize,

~~i would see people~~ as among
fragments of the future

quidditatively

~~so to those who deny that some being is contingent~~
~~should be~~ exposed to torments til they concede that
~~it is possible for them not to be tormented~~

stasis = civil war ~~community~~

paint blue flower red

build new world in shell of old

the form of ~~the~~ slave

apropos of amor fati

do you have another pinion

ought to be a real red flag

 bike chain snapped
at adeline & ashby

washed my hands &
walked to bart

bruce killed his
roommate in an argument

david foster wallace suicide.

to shape the object requires that
one attain a proper distance from it.

the question is ~~proper~~ relation.

i called ithaca self storage.

the woman said
'it's a wonderful day at ithaca self storage!'

i found a receipt in a book with
today's date.

hurry, as if there were a fire!

came home, footsore,
read
ecce homo.

time entered economy,
economy's libidinal.

every time two persons are together,
mitra's the third person.

we intuit ourselves only as we are inwardly
affected by ourselves.

there ~~■■■~~ remains the space ~~■■■■~~ the body
~~■■■■■■■■■■■■■~~
occupied, can't.
and this ~~■■■~~ be removed.

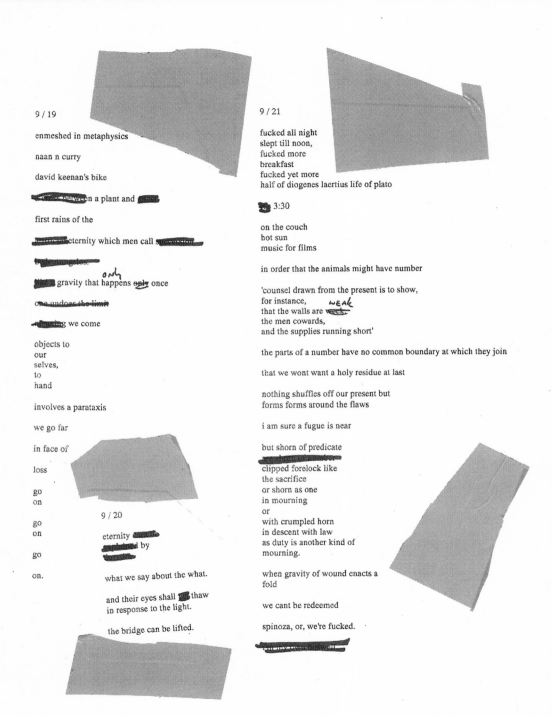

9 / 19

enmeshed in metaphysics

naan n curry

david keenan's bike

~~between~~ en a plant and ~~~~

first rains of the

~~~~eternity which men call ~~~~

~~~~

~~~~ gravity that happens ~~only~~ once   only

~~one undoes the limit~~

~~~~ we come

objects to
our
selves,
to
hand

involves a parataxis

we go far

in face of

loss

go
on

go
on

go

on.

9 / 20

eternity ~~~~
~~~~ by

what we say about the what.

and their eyes shall ~~~~ thaw
in response to the light.

the bridge can be lifted.

9 / 21

fucked all night
slept till noon,
fucked more
breakfast
fucked yet more
half of diogenes laertius life of plato

3:30

on the couch
hot sun
music for films

in order that the animals might have number

'counsel drawn from the present is to show,
for instance,                 weak
that the walls are ~~weak~~
the men cowards,
and the supplies running short'

the parts of a number have no common boundary at which they join

that we wont want a holy residue at last

nothing shuffles off our present but
forms forms around the flaws

i am sure a fugue is near

but shorn of predicate
~~~~
clipped forelock like
the sacrifice
or shorn as one
in mourning
or
with crumpled horn
in descent with law
as duty is another kind of
mourning.

when gravity of wound enacts a
fold

we cant be redeemed

spinoza, or, we're fucked.

~~~~

2 conversations ▓▓▓▓▓ moved to ▓▓ trash.

a lot of clotted filters

▓▓▓▓▓▓▓ about canessa

▓▓▓▓ it was LONG

▓▓▓▓ of love

▓▓▓▓▓▓▓▓▓▓▓▓▓▓ 1 book today

▓▓▓▓▓▓▓ the question

▓▓▓▓▓ has ▓ tremendous right

since figure is nothing but ▓▓▓▓▓▓▓▓
▓▓▓▓▓▓▓▓▓▓▓▓▓▓▓
▓▓▓▓▓▓▓▓▓▓▓ negation,
▓▓▓▓▓▓▓▓

▓▓▓▓▓▓▓,
why remember it?

no thing is in form of is

no gnosis here's alas all apodictic,
more like deictic

▓▓▓▓▓ congeals

at ▓▓ intemporal kernel

pretext for poverty's metaxu's
~~pretext~~ &
there's not a thing to hold

that love like langue in sway of what's no proper

but underneath a law that all
burlesques a proper
propter hoc

our people is our people
i.e. cash is not the vector

a politics of sufficiency of utterance in this
milieu
▓▓▓ aint gonna fucking cut it

all which has been fastened may be loosened

all that is solid melts into
us

sown into the instruments of time

ducats thy monad
pli selon pli

wit riddim his diffrence
sunder the plan
set silvae at sevens, at
sixes & sevens
and suck up the juices that
only keep coming.

sync up perversions but
differ in judgments,
if phone's fold,
if cash his catachresis
what we do sans transcendental
ego,
who paid for thy grundrisse lady?

see the beauty,
touch the magic

moments of the notion that
bare eimi bore

& that jerusalem is

& zion all evacuate save
as the form of home

say babylon besieges babylon
gone west with sun
as berkeley said
thus i refute
yer monist shit

a point is that which has no part

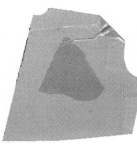

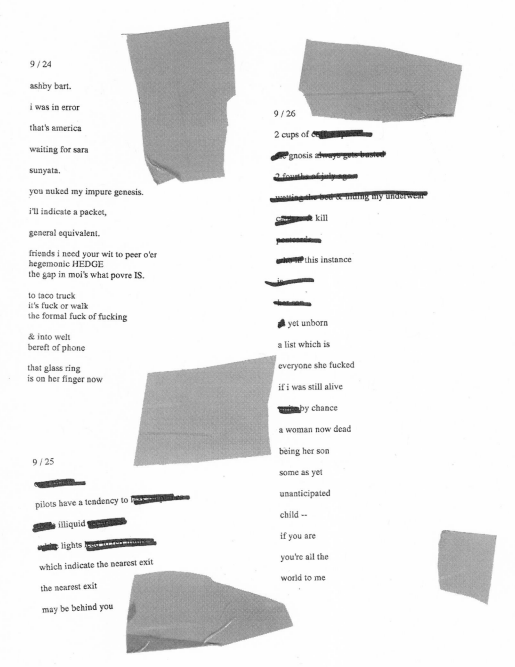

9 / 24

ashby bart.

i was in error

that's america

waiting for sara

sunyata.

you nuked my impure genesis.

i'll indicate a packet,

general equivalent.

friends i need your wit to peer o'er
hegemonic HEDGE
the gap in moi's what povre IS.

to taco truck
it's fuck or walk
the formal fuck of fucking

& into welt
bereft of phone

that glass ring
is on her finger now

9 / 25

~~illiquid~~

pilots have a tendency to ~~fuck~~

~~illiquid~~

~~lights~~ lights ~~illiquid~~

which indicate the nearest exit

the nearest exit

may be behind you

9 / 26

2 cups of c~~~~

~~the gnosis always gets busted~~

~~2 fourths of july again~~

~~wetting the bed & hiding my underwear~~

c~~~~ kill

~~postcards~~

~~the~~ this instance

~~is~~

~~her son~~

yet unborn

a list which is

everyone she fucked

if i was still alive

~~which~~ by chance

a woman now dead

being her son

some as yet

unanticipated

child --

if you are

you're all the

world to me

9 / 28

~~9/26~~ wedding ~~day~~

~~is~~ gone threadbare

~~after industry~~

~~gone of encounter~~

to undo ~~some~~ genre that we are

~~but how will it happen~~ in this country, or

~~what can i do?~~

~~she copied out~~ the mantra

gate gate paragate parasamgate bodhi svaha

~~[gone gone gone beyond gone completely beyond]~~

9 / 27

window 27 for a reimbursement

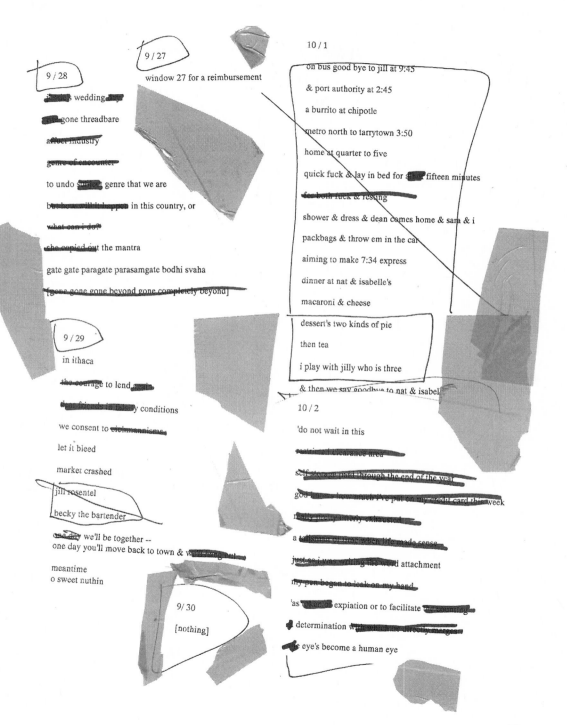

9 / 29

in ithaca

~~the courage to lend again~~

~~dear friends in many~~ conditions

we consent to ~~eichmannisms~~

let it bleed

market crashed

jill rosentel

becky the bartender

~~one day~~ we'll be together --
one day you'll move back to town & ~~we'll forget that~~

meantime
o sweet nuthin

9/ 30

[nothing]

10 / 1

on bus good bye to jill at 9:45

& port authority at 2:45

a burrito at chipotle

metro north to tarrytown 3:50

home at quarter to five

quick fuck & lay in bed for ~~just~~ fifteen minutes

~~for both fuck & resting~~

shower & dress & dean comes home & sara & i

packbags & throw em in the car

aiming to make 7:34 express

dinner at nat & isabelle's

macaroni & cheese

dessert's two kinds of pie

then tea

i play with jilly who is three

& then we say goodbye to nat & isabel

10 / 2

'do not wait in this

~~restricted clearance area~~

~~self storage paid through the end of the year~~

~~god knows how much i've put on my credit card this week~~

~~really already overly exhausted~~

~~a different mood where life made sense~~

~~just as i was watching the word~~ attachment

~~my pen began to leak on my hand~~

'as ~~a kind of~~ expiation or to facilitate ~~the something~~

~~a~~ determination ~~which would be directly analogous~~

~~the~~ eye's become a human eye

IX

plunged however ~~~~~~~~
into cares

~~labor shelter~~

~~store item~~

~~~ thy law is burnt

~~~~~~~~~~~ engrafted

water thief

~~~~ enonce

deviser ~~of voice~~
~~and of its hearer~~
~~and~~ of himself

~~friends help poor~~ o'er
~~dangerous hedge~~

labor univocal in the ~~~~~~~~
~~~~~ roses ~~~~~~~~~~~~~
from the gardens of ~~~~~~~~~~
~~~~~~~~~~~~~~~~~~~~~~~
~~sign of effective demand~~

da~~~~~~~~ taught you lore like
~~~~~~~~~~~ of Denmark

mcmansion of clean stone

time's deracine
past's protege,
        ~~~~~ cortege of sortilege
            ~~~~~ like ~

~~~ debt ~~~~~~~~~~~~~~~~~~~
~~~~~~~~~~~~ of ~~~~~ "

~~~~~~~~~~~~~
~~~~~~~~~~~~~~~~~~~~~
~~~~~~~~~~~~~~ which ~~~~~~~
david ~~~~~~~~
~~~ workday went all ~~~~~

~~~~ in ~~~~~~ the genre ~~~~~~~~~~
~~~~~~~~~~~~~

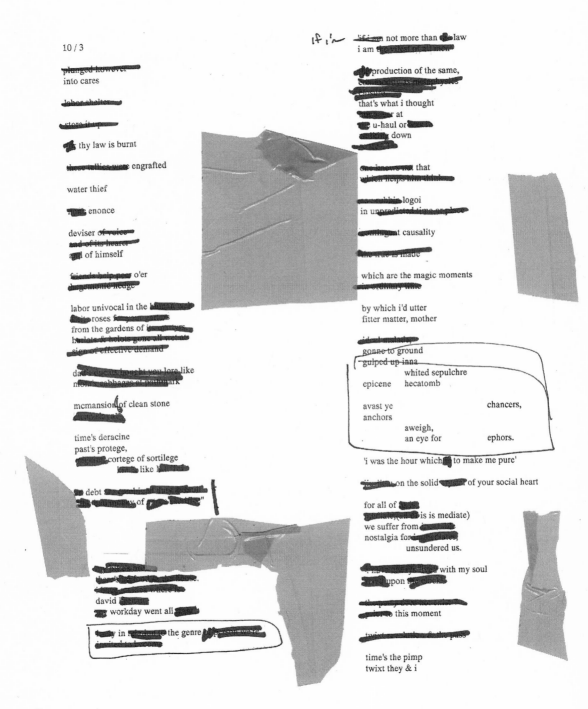

If i'm

~~if i am~~ not more than ~~the~~ law
i am ~~~~~~~~~~~~~~~~

~~the~~ production of the same,
~~~~~~~~~~~~~~~~~~~~~~~
~~~~~~~~~
that's what i thought
~~~~~~~~ at
~~~ u-haul or ~~~~~
~~~~~~ down

~~~~~~~~~~ that
~~~~~~~~~~~~~~

~~~~~~~~ logoi
in unpredicted ~~~~~~~~~~~~

~~~~~~~~~ causality
~~~~~~~~~~~~~

which are the magic moments
~~~~~~~~~~~~

by which i'd utter
fitter matter, mother

~~~~~~~~~~~~
gonne to ground
gulped up inna
            whited sepulchre
epicene   hecatomb

avast ye   chancers,
anchors
        aweigh,
        an eye for   ephors.

'i was the hour which~ to make me pure'

~~~~~~~~ on the solid ~~~~~ of your social heart

for all of ~~~~~
~~~~~~~~~(this is mediate)
we suffer from ~~~~~~~~~~
nostalgia for ~~~~~~~~~~~~
            unsundered us.

~~~~~~~~~~~~~ with my soul
~~~~ upon ~~~~~~~

~~~~~~~~~~~~~~~
~~~~~ to this moment

~~~~~~~~~~~~~~~~~~~~

time's the pimp
twixt they & i

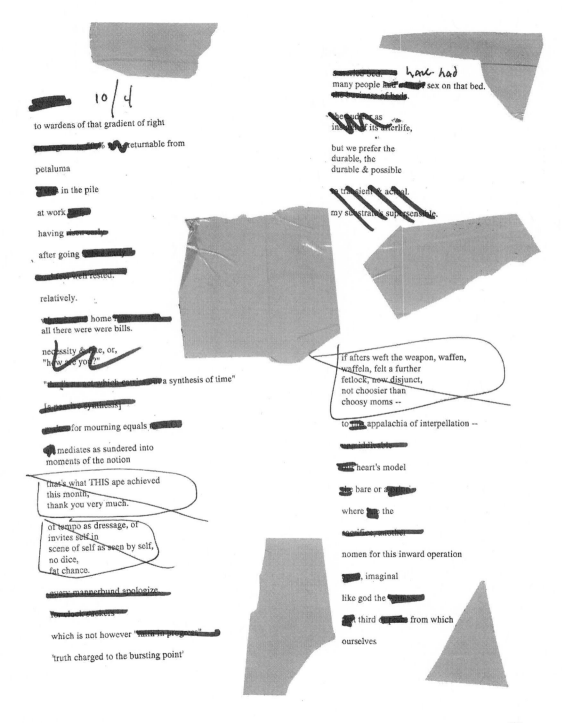

10/4

to wardens of that gradient of right

returnable from

petaluma

in the pile

at work

having

after going

well rested.

relatively.

home
all there were were bills.

necessity & one, or,
"how are you?"

"which carries a synthesis of time"

[a passive synthesis]

for mourning equals

mediates as sundered into
moments of the notion

that's what THIS ape achieved
this month,
thank you very much.

of tempo as dressage, of
invites self in
scene of self as seen by self,
no dice,
fat chance.

every mannerbund apologize.

which is not however "faith in progress"

'truth charged to the bursting point'

have had
many people had sex on that bed.

as
ins of its afterlife,

but we prefer the
durable, the
durable & possible

transient & actual.

my substrate's supersensible.

if afters weft the weapon, waffen,
waffeln, felt a further
fetlock, now disjunct,
not choosier than
choosy moms --

to the appalachia of interpellation --

heart's model

bare or a

where the

nomen for this inward operation

, imaginal

like god the

third from which

ourselves

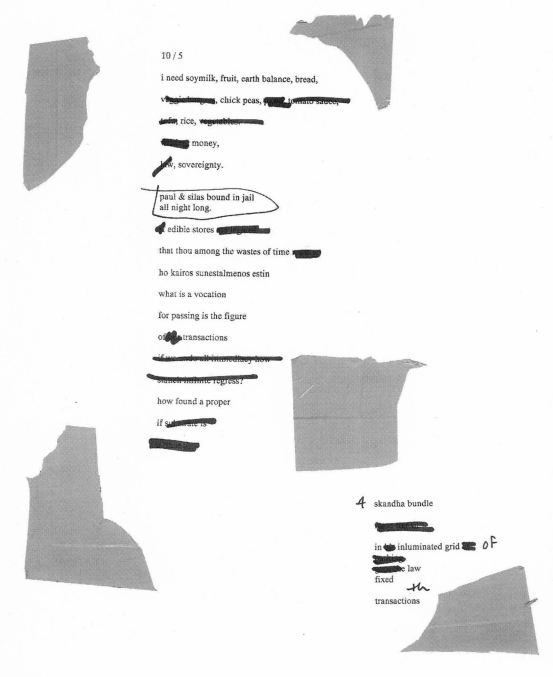

10 / 5

i need soymilk, fruit, earth balance, bread,

~~veggie burgers~~, chick peas, ~~████~~ ~~tomato sauce,~~

~~tofu~~, rice, ~~vegetables~~ ~~████~~

~~████~~ money,

law, sovereignty.

paul & silas bound in jail
all night long.

edible stores ~~████~~

that thou among the wastes of time ~~████~~

ho kairos sunestalmenos estin

what is a vocation

for passing is the figure

of ~~██~~ transactions

~~if we undo all immediacy how~~

~~stanch infinite regress?~~

how found a proper

if su~~███~~ate is

~~████~~

4 skandha bundle

~~████~~

in ~~██~~ inluminated grid ~~██~~ of

~~██~~ ~~██~~e law
fixed
th
transactions

rampant technical difficulties

one hundred and thirteen dollars

what do other people eat?

remembering to do this things is labor.

both doing & remembrance

'chaotic' milk industry

a kind of ultimate florin

seeing one face in the signs of all coinage

labor is the censored chapter

whose laid up in

████████████

████ substance

time, crypt, labor, money, tragedy,
translation, commodity,
sublime, irony, distance, technics,
jointure,
            struggle,

point, punctum, stigme.
now, nunc, nun.

therefore circles are grades of ████

████████ necessity.

now i'm at doe.

no spesial reason to go home.

i dont know what work is & i have never.

how place became space,
homogenous because homogenized.
like milk,
like milk & math.

vestige, echo, remnant

████ as ictus
        ████ set by the hand.

overlapping hums & ████████

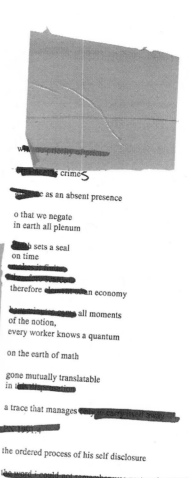

w██████████████████

████████ crime**s**

████ as an absent presence

o that we negate
in earth all plenum

████ sets a seal
on time
██████████████
██████████████
therefore ██████ an economy

████████████ all moments
of the notion,
every worker knows a quantum

on the earth of math

gone mutually translatable
in t██████████

a trace that manages ████████████████

████ 1991.4

the ordered process of his self disclosure

the word i could not remember was protrepticus

██t there was when he was not

punctilinear optics in nuce

all points contract to monad of the ducat,
        kid --

████ posterity lasts████ until
the next mass is said

if we are silent, stones cry out

memory's the gallows

t██████ occasion for idolatry

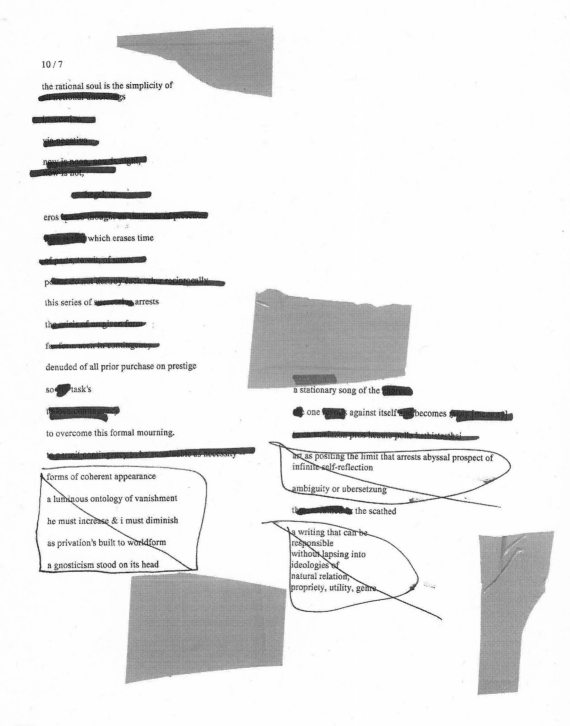

the rational soul is the simplicity of

now is not,

eros

which erases time

this series of arrests

denuded of all prior purchase on prestige

so task's

to overcome this formal mourning.

a stationary song of the

one against itself becomes

art as positing the limit that arrests abyssal prospect of
infinite self-reflection

ambiguity or ubersetzung

the scathed

forms of coherent appearance

a luminous ontology of vanishment

he must increase & i must diminish

as privation's built to worldform

a gnosticism stood on its head

a writing that can be
responsible
without lapsing into
ideologies of
natural relation;
propriety, utility, genre

10 / 8

poor, bare, forked
fucked &
filth though thou art
                    how hollow heart,
how halo,

an inedibler precinct of
my patrimony

operates a
                    capture farm
form's forcing house --

is moved or set or shaped or else
effaced
by "cold command"

implicature in signal ducat hub yields
                    verum factum
amor fati

futures markets

for the way   does not exist

who reconciled discipline & grace

if a horse in his elation should cry out
i am beautiful
it would be bearable.

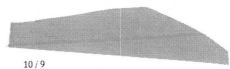

10 / 9

i were cunning's "agent"

soymilk & shave cream

while i am strong i'm

failing o a

wrecche

for the point ~~███████████~~

is the beginning of one &

the end of another

but if you consider one point as

two

an arrest or pause is

necessary

if the same point is to ~~███~~

begin ~~██~~ and end

~~███████~~

the self's a cloister of remembered sounds

and of sounds so far forgotten like her voice

that they return unrecognized

intuitions which are stations but

~~█~~ on what via

what ~~does dialectics~~ map

~~███~~ ctly?

what if i'm ~~██~~ sick passenger?

~~█~~ e time that moves forward &

th ~~█~~ time that moves back

i'd intended, but
what closes gap twixt
image in the mind &
fulfilled object is
labor

having lost the forms & faith
in forms

we have ~~████~~ only
prosody,

a houseless
meter

bare yard broke fence

deracinated
us

~~█████████████████████████~~

~~temporal revanchism~~

~~█~~ voluntaristic individual ethics only
validate ~~ourselves~~
~~to ourselves~~
~~████████~~ t a form of
predicate narcissus,

~~commodity lotto.~~

either ladder or else
indra's net
value descends or it's
autopoietic in its manufacture,
guess which i believe it.

the ~~way~~ in wh ~~ich~~ we lose ~~██~~ r own powers
for w ~~██~~ t we ~~█~~ e recognized t ~~█~~ autho ~~█~~

ho ~~█~~ do we overcome the impossibl ~~█~~ wish
to ~~█~~ e governed by necessity?

an ~~█~~ other aspect of formal
mourning,
or u ~~█~~ building
(~~██~~ au)

had we but a basis,
~~this is archimedes point~~

~~but when it's known~~
~~████████ conventional~~
~~██████~~
~~█████████████~~ cessary,
how then may we vest?

watch out for the darkness

o steresis

o privation's ██████ ████

████ ███ ██████ most discreet,

a tear's ██ ███████ ██ █ █████

██ ██ ██ a fine and private place,

██ ████████ ██ ████, Orestes,

shorn of predicates &

capable

██ █ pay you █████████

in ██████ █ ██ bride is clad   *laude*

the integral of velocity represents

my esemplastic power

comes undone amidst

amidst

the remnant or the residue which is erotic fodder

so was bleibt maps us as us &

channels trieb to telos

time's pure hope

so no thing's left of me but
action of that tearing

so i'm not sundered but
that sundering itself

bereft perhaps

dear kid if
you're a lamb they'll

often roast you in his houses.

████ as a figure for
return of what's one's own
in a disguis-ed
guise

as supple as a supplement

was bleibt ist
██ cinder of the sender
██████ ████████ ██ ████████
██ █████ ██ ███ ██████

remembrance as ██████████
██ persistent labor

██████ enters juncture,
██████ ███████

██████ ██ ██████████,
████████ as this reduction.

if i was where i would be
then i'd be where i am now
there where i must be
where i would be i cannot'

'a philosophy linked to the hangman'

machines is that what
breaks a flow
to figure out a step
or to articulate
time space by
way of contrast

"to abolish interval is also to abolish strategy."

~~chronos~~ ~~when the nick and joint of time~~

chronos~~~~ that in which ~~time~~ is kairos
~~and~~ kairos ~~~~ that in which ~~time is~~ ~~the~~ chronos

small

~~eroticized thought~~

"the lack of ~~coincidence~~ between
knowledge & being"

time yields no forms

our bloom is gone. we are the fruit thereof.

so stasis is that status
hence this stasimon,
~~~~

chronothesis posited in enonce of an i

this remnant or reduction

orphan of phenomenon

brought low

labor in train to
~~~~
gravity libido

asymptote to pictures

to ~~~~ gap in which all work is dumped

~~gap of the ~~ ~~~~ ~~gap of love~~ ~~~~

moment as the trauma of relentless loss

gainst which no stave

~~~~ ~~~~ ~~cannot think is~~

for here were earth &
sky made sundered

& fro' out

maternal fold the
rotten reproduction ~~~~

of who eats & we are lacking

~~~~ lack & love & labor & we
need to eat

& we reduced we
broken from our kin &
they inflict this grammar of a us on us
of ~~~~

~~identity with one who flush or shorn~~

the present as ~~~~
~~a clasp or hasp~~
a hinge or joint or nick,
articulated nought

must ironic distance evacuate the right to affect

revolutionary = bodhisattva

in contradistinction to aesthetic is
communicable & weaponizd

packet to affect the sense
            enter the conjuncture of

paralysis, arrest, stasis, stop

to genres of the fuckable.

you anticipate the lapse the actual will be

we stand on edge & we acquit

~~a reduction, to ~~ ~~~~

communicable quanta

my brother's my half brother & so's his.

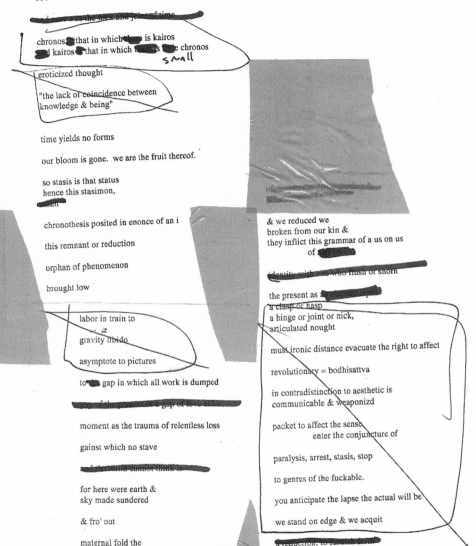

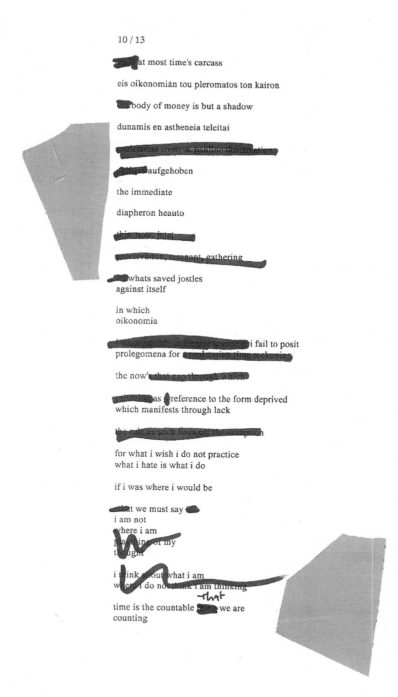

▬▬at most time's carcass

eis oikonomián tou pleromatos ton kairon

▬▬body of money is but a shadow

dunamis en astheneia teleitai

▬▬▬▬▬▬▬▬▬▬▬▬▬▬▬▬▬▬▬▬▬▬▬

▬▬▬aufgehoben

the immediate

diapheron heauto

▬▬▬▬▬▬▬▬▬▬

▬▬▬▬▬▬, remnant, gathering

▬▬whats saved jostles
against itself

in which
oikonomia

▬▬▬▬▬▬▬▬▬▬▬▬▬▬▬▬▬i fail to posit
prolegomena for ▬▬▬▬▬▬▬▬▬▬▬▬▬

the now'▬▬▬▬▬▬▬▬▬▬▬▬

▬▬▬▬▬as ▬reference to the form deprived
which manifests through lack

▬▬▬▬▬▬▬▬▬▬▬▬▬▬▬▬▬▬

for what i wish i do not practice
what i hate is what i do

if i was where i would be

▬▬▬▬t we must say ▬▬
i am not
where i am
▬▬▬▬ing of my
thought

i think about what i am
where i do not think i am thinking —that
time is the countable ▬▬▬ we are
counting

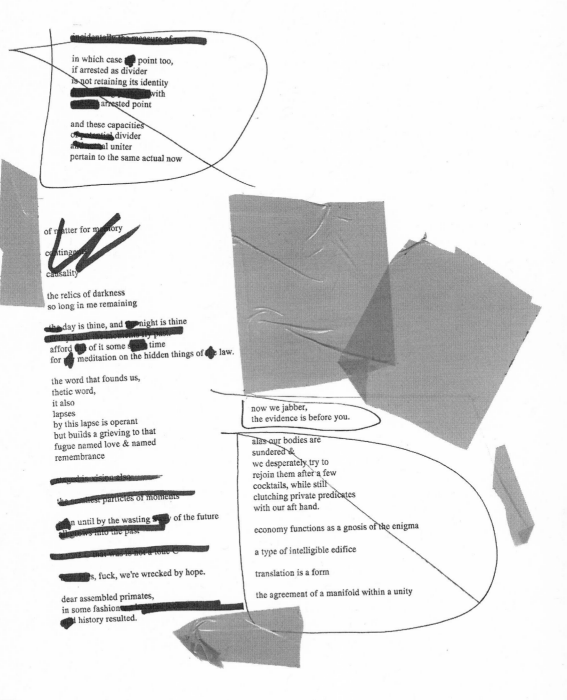

incidentally the measure of rest

in which case ⬛ point too,
if arrested as divider
is not retaining its identity
⬛⬛⬛ with
⬛⬛ arrested point

and these capacities
of potential divider
and ⬛⬛al uniter
pertain to the same actual now

of matter for memory

contingent

causality

the relics of darkness
so long in me remaining

the day is thine, and ⬛ night is thine
⬛⬛⬛⬛⬛⬛⬛⬛⬛
afford ⬛ of it some s⬛ time
for ⬛ meditation on the hidden things of ⬛ law.

the word that founds us,
thetic word,
it also
lapses
by this lapse is operant
but builds a grieving to that
fugue named love & named
remembrance

⬛⬛⬛⬛⬛⬛⬛⬛⬛

the ⬛⬛⬛est particles of moments

⬛⬛n until by the wasting ⬛⬛y of the future
it grows into the past

⬛⬛⬛⬛⬛⬛ that was is not a tone ⬛

⬛⬛s, fuck, we're wrecked by hope.

dear assembled primates,
in some fashion ⬛⬛⬛⬛⬛⬛
⬛l history resulted.

now we jabber,
the evidence is before you.

alas our bodies are
sundered &
we desperately try to
rejoin them after a few
cocktails, while still
clutching private predicates
with our aft hand.

economy functions as a gnosis of the enigma

a type of intelligible edifice

translation is a form

the agreement of a manifold within a unity

we carried you
in ▮ arms
▮▮▮▮▮▮▮▮ day

▮▮▮ to ▮▮▮▮g fire

the ▮▮▮▮▮▮▮ of ▮▮▮▮▮▮▮▮
▮▮▮▮▮▮▮▮ ▮▮▮▮▮

▮ adequation to the thing ▮▮▮▮▮▮▮▮
▮▮▮▮▮▮

▮▮▮▮▮▮▮▮ at the moment that ▮▮▮▮▮▮▮▮ time
observes the ▮▮▮▮▮▮▮▮▮▮▮▮▮▮▮

▮ place of the becoming ▮▮▮▮▮▮ *of*

▮▮▮▮▮▮▮▮▮▮▮ ▮▮▮▮▮▮▮▮▮▮

the law that can unfold out of occasion,
▮▮▮▮▮▮▮ of a sundered metrics
▮▮▮▮▮▮▮▮▮▮ ▮▮▮▮▮▮▮▮ into history
▮▮▮▮▮▮

so that love is reason ▮▮▮▮
and reflection's always amorous

judith, god speaks at last

but one does not make the other come,
one lets it come by preparing for ▮▮▮▮▮▮

the sister's lunar voice

a foretaste of mourning

the memory of what he forgets

▮▮ stasis is a state & ▮▮like
a stand within the state
of a dissent adelphous
or of ▮▮▮▮▮▮ ▮▮▮▮▮ ~~discord~~ *descent*

but if we take up bonds another way
▮▮▮▮▮ ▮▮▮▮▮▮▮▮▮▮ & in rights
▮▮ property

if ▮▮▮▮▮▮ our
reduction is that lack that makes us
reach across --

▮▮▮ ▮▮▮▮▮▮ ▮▮▮▮

▮▮▮▮▮ the gate

what do i do with all this freedom?

▮▮▮▮▮▮▮▮ ▮▮▮▮▮▮▮ when
i'm toward the end

en route to work
& waiting for a sign,

for an assignment.

'they also serve who only stand and wait.'

KAIPOE (3), & due measure, proportion, fitness, Hes. etc.: παρὰ τόπ beyond measure, Aesch. etc.: μετὰ τοῦ καιροῦ. Lat. justo ε.αμ; Xen.   II of place. a vital part of the body, ἵκετο καιρον, Eur.   III of time. the point of time, the proper time or season of action, exact or critical time, (οft opposed in this), καιρος ... time and tide wait for no man; Pind.; ... to settle times & by. There is τηκει Eur.; καιρον λαμβάνειν time; έχει καιρον to be in season, Id.:-καιρος έστι c. inf., it is time to do, fit, etc.

FIG. 2.—Detail of the Leviathan.

11 / 9

Nature ~~appears~~ ~~only~~ as j~~udgment~~
~~but this would take us too far afield here~~

In bed all day

~~interesting~~

~~prophylactic sick days~~

~~understaffing~~

run down & ~~~~

κατεχον ~~The Retainer~~

~~who~~ who holds ~~back / retards~~
the flowe
~~of history~~

toward reign of ~~antichrist~~

~~thinking of~~ entropy as
sorting ghosts

~~as Maxwell~~

enact ~~~~

leviathan and i~~con~~
~~the anti-christ~~

~~genealogy of~~ figure
rose against us

~~power~~ without ~~an~~ image,
but our matrix i~~n~~ ~~the author~~

~~protestant versions~~
~~included~~ for election else

~~~~

▓ we preterite
passed over ▓▓▓▓▓▓▓

▓▓▓▓ to understand the concept

"traces of ▓ true ▓▓▓▓▓▓"

▓▓▓▓▓▓▓▓▓ common
in a way not <u>metaphorical</u>

<u>mimetic</u> --

                    Blaser, Collis,
Virno,
            John Clare,

Marx, Thompson, Polanyi, Winstanley,
            Mauss, Blake

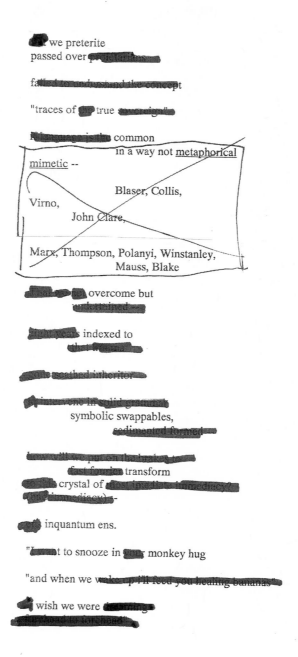

▓▓▓▓▓ overcome but
▓▓▓▓▓▓▓▓

▓▓▓▓▓▓ indexed to
▓▓▓▓▓▓▓

▓▓▓ ▓▓▓▓▓ inheritor

▓▓▓▓▓▓▓ in solid grammar
symbolic swappables,
            ▓▓▓▓▓▓▓ ▓▓▓▓▓

▓▓▓▓▓▓ we put on that blanket
fast fourier transform
        crystal of ▓▓▓▓ ▓▓▓▓▓ immediacy/
▓▓▓▓▓ ▓▓▓▓ -

▓▓▓ inquantum ens.

"▓▓▓ ▓ to snooze in ▓▓▓ monkey hug

"and when we wake up I'll feed you healing bananas

▓▓ wish we were ▓▓▓▓▓▓▓
▓▓▓▓▓▓ to forehead ▓

the faucet is ▮▮▮▮▮
▮▮▮▮▮▮▮▮▮▮▮ stop it

▮ endeavor of ▮▮▮▮▮
▮▮▮▮▮▮▮▮▮▮

▮▮▮▮▮▮▮▮▮▮▮▮
▮▮▮▮▮▮▮ decaying sense

▮▮▮ where speech is not,
▮▮▮▮▮▮▮▮▮▮▮▮▮▮▮

those ▮▮▮▮▮▮▮▮▮▮▮

(▮▮▮▮▮▮▮ spirits)

▮▮▮▮ incorporeal ▮▮▮▮▮▮▮▮▮▮▮▮

▮▮▮▮▮▮▮▮▮▮▮▮▮▮
▮▮▮▮▮▮▮▮▮▮▮▮ that is to say
so much as would be given for the use
▮▮▮▮▮▮▮▮▮▮▮▮▮▮▮▮▮▮
▮▮▮▮▮▮▮▮▮▮▮▮▮▮▮▮▮▮

                    ▮▮▮▮▮

"▮▮▮▮▮▮▮▮▮▮▮▮▮▮ of t▮▮▮▮▮▮"

"▮▮▮▮▮▮▮▮▮▮▮▮ obligation i▮▮▮▮▮▮▮
▮▮▮▮▮▮▮▮▮▮▮ obligation, perpetual ▮▮▮▮▮▮▮"

▮▮▮▮ forth in filth in
        filth & destitution
as inflict▮ on ▮ one whom accidents
        have rendered ▮▮▮▮▮
▮▮▮▮▮▮▮▮▮▮▮▮▮▮ riven▮
▮▮▮▮▮▮▮▮▮▮▮▮▮▮▮▮▮▮
predicates   'gainst▮
▮▮▮▮▮▮▮▮ neighbors, hence
loneliness of ▮▮▮▮▮▮▮ labor or of
▮▮▮▮▮▮▮▮▮▮▮▮
measure ▮▮▮▮ like the spirit walks ▮▮▮▮▮
▮▮▮▮▮
with seven ▮▮▮▮ kin
to batter down your door
        a▮▮▮▮ name for interest ▮▮▮▮▮
also --

~~Love is simple.~~
~~Sense~~ is ~~real~~

                    I owe and want the
means to pay.

the ~~This~~ year is catching up with me.

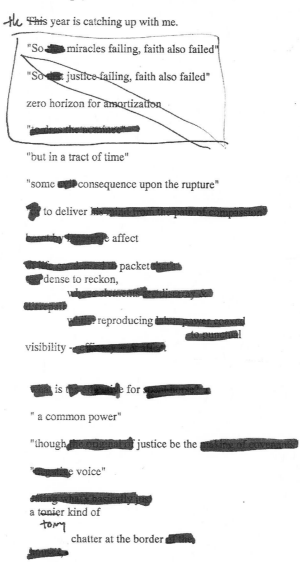

"So ▓ miracles failing, faith also failed"

"So ▓ justice failing, faith also failed"

zero horizon for amortization

"▓▓▓▓▓▓▓▓▓▓▓▓"

"but in a tract of time"

"some ▓▓ consequence upon the rupture"

▓ to deliver ▓▓▓▓▓▓▓▓▓▓▓▓▓▓▓▓▓▓▓

▓▓▓▓▓ ▓▓▓▓▓▓ affect

▓▓▓▓▓▓▓▓▓▓▓▓ packet ▓▓▓▓
▓ dense to reckon,
            ▓▓▓▓▓▓▓▓▓▓ ▓▓▓▓▓▓▓▓▓
▓▓▓▓▓▓▓
        ▓▓▓▓ reproducing ▓▓▓▓▓▓▓▓▓▓▓▓
                        ▓▓▓▓▓▓▓
visibility - ▓▓▓▓▓▓▓▓▓▓▓▓

        ▓▓ is ▓▓▓▓▓▓▓ for ▓▓▓▓▓▓▓▓

" a common power"

"though ▓▓▓▓▓▓▓▓▓▓ justice be the ▓▓▓▓▓▓▓▓▓▓▓▓

"▓▓▓▓▓▓ voice"

▓▓▓▓▓▓▓▓▓▓▓▓▓▓▓▓
a ~~tonier~~ *tony* kind of

        chatter at the border ▓▓▓▓
▓▓▓▓▓

▓▓▓▓▓▓▓▓▓▓▓▓▓▓▓▓

▮▮▮ like a clock

team up to knit ▮ shut

▮▮▮▮ ▮▮s ▮ apperception

▮▮▮▮ gainst imaginary traffic

▮▮▮▮▮▮▮▮ of ▮▮▮▮-self
▮▮▮▮▮▮▮▮ who
stymied formed a figure for ▮▮
incoherence
▮▮ folie a deux we stabilize

▮▮▮▮ won't miss the rotted trash & soap
▮▮▮ love my hands

a sad ▮▮▮▮▮▮▮▮ & bound
▮▮▮▮▮▮▮ ▮▮▮▮▮▮
portion of ▮ actually descent into the
yet to come

▮▮▮▮▮▮▮ this destitution

dust & ▮▮ mote of ▮ might

(a mite)

           a mute

mate

     meet

          mite

mote   mute.

who ▮ waits the ▮▮▮▮ word as one
▮▮▮ in hope of ▮▮▮▮▮

pardon ▮▮▮▮▮ died ▮▮▮▮▮▮▮

when ▮▮ lights
▮▮▮▮ to fail,
        you write
mid glitch
▮▮▮▮▮▮,
for ▮▮ dead have saved the living

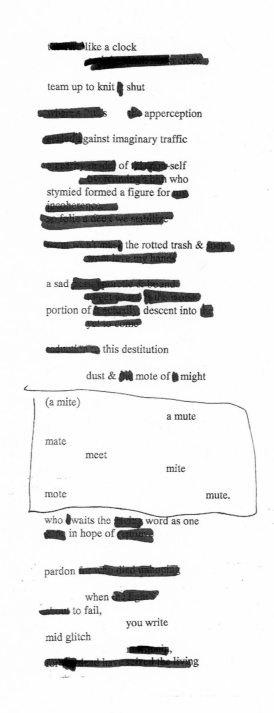

a ███████

"██████████ to say ██████
    the ███t joyful,
███ ███ here in mourning,
    ██████████████████

█████████ love past understanding"

██████████████

███ which is imperishable says

        ██ this that fatal
lord within us

            ███████████████

What █████ I write in lieu of letter
        I could write her and cannot.

████████ aware
        ████████████████
of ████████████████
        ████ debt and the █████.

"███████████████████

██ disgrace of price"

████████████████████████████

amidst ████████████
        ████████████████████

enigma of epistle ████

        ████████████████ est negatio

haven lost 'em what
        else does the frozen
father function

                    "a forged dad"

    wood or word or works

    when they say this is a great book about
                America
    what can they have meant?

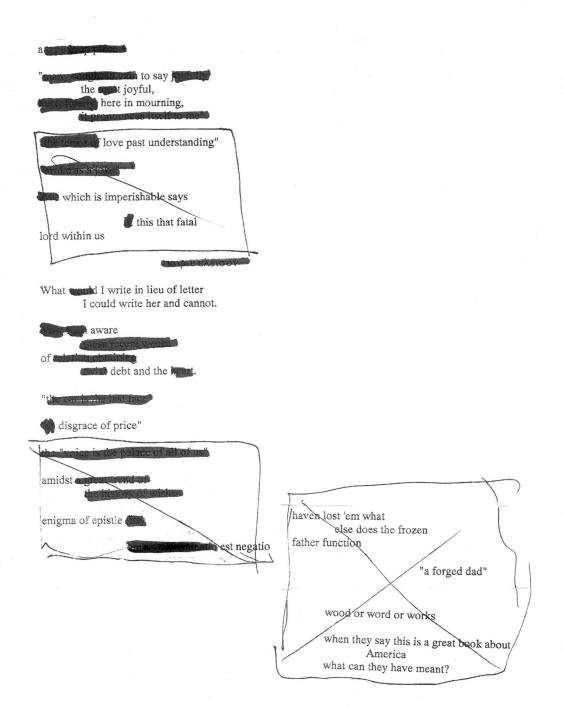

                         "if you cannot
give a million
        you can give a widow's mite"

        till social will
sublates the nude electorate it's just

another 9 / 11 booty call

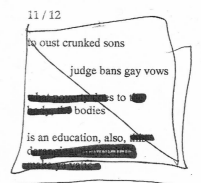

to oust crunked sons

        judge bans gay vows

~~that contributes to the~~
~~helpless~~ bodies

is an education, also, ~~this~~
~~detention newspaper~~
~~make you wait~~

lay a lion limb gainst me

            I barely
slept last night.   My stomach's in
knots. I cant see out of this.

I lay awake in bed
thinking this is my kingdom.

Can you fuck ~~someone~~

~~"live vicariously through no one"~~

~~cast~~ your bread upon the waters,
~~what's the other fucking option.~~

~~i am being slowly destroyed~~

~~spiro agnew.~~

~~✎~~ time strength cash and ~~patience~~

~~the department's in receivership~~

~~where's authority, responsibility,~~
~~legitimacy, sovereignty.~~

~~●~~ question of whence vest

~~contract & covenant~~

        ~~author & actor~~

~~personality as essence of~~
~~citizen~~

~~place, name, birthdate/~~

~~who could~~ ~~act~~ the citizen
~~in absence of a formal meaning,~~

as ~~a~~ law whose
~~positive's suspended~~   ~~human particularly as a~~
~~practice of remediation~~
                                            ~~a~~ remnant ~~here~~   ~~gone down into~~
                                                        ~~sickness~~ ~~unconscious~~

~~& this concept's~~ key
                                            ~~empty, empty   empty   empty   empty~~

"And I and I and I and ~~some strange face~~
~~Wretched -- Solitary -- Here~~

~~the secret room~~   ~~humility of goodmorning is~~
                                            ~~engaged~~ passivity that
~~____~~ in the local ~~landscape~~"   ~~permits something to happen~~

~~not invisible but nondescript~~

                                            ~~foreclosing~~ expectation ~~lets~~
"~~a private company called~~ covenant"   ~~itself foreclose~~   ~~possibility~~

"deep packet inspection"   ~~framing of gestell.~~

        That for us there is no   in absence of ~~already on~~
everyday.   ~~solution what.~~

"attempts to buy   ~~is what is present susceptible~~
~~property rights on the open market~~"   ~~to~~ inversion?

mate / mete / mite / mote / mute   ~~what can it become?~~

~~____ ____ Wassham~~   "~~what will it have been~~ to
~~_____~~   remember ~~this~~ rather than to
                                            ~~have it as experience?~~

~~would give us~~
~~complete mastery over the physical world~~   ~~because of one you will not~~ be
                                            a witness
~~things & bits ____ such as the hand~~   (~~having down perfected~~
                                            ~~humanity of the perfections of~~
~~_____~~   ~~judgement~~ or ~~only~~ a survivor)

                                            ~~imagination, likeness, sympathy,~~
                                            ~~_____~~

                                            build a legacy for
                                            ~~what inheritors?~~

~~robes & what to break~~

depending on the tense of utterance

"~~_____ take title~~"

~~the _____ jects~~ point to

empty center
~~aporetic~~

from this vantage --

o~~_____ platform~~
four in a row
in the same posture
looking at their cellphone,
locked in gesture
as in frieze
as Danteville

~~noli me tangere~~

~~minimal works of~~
~~_____ analogy clarity~~
~~via reduction~~
                    & how
am i living,
        fake chicken patty & ▌Tecate

for <u>this</u> "Egyptian" ~~--~~

~~everything belongs to me~~
        because I am poor"

~~_____~~ to be
born again th~~_____ of you~~

~~g_____ got _____~~ in
        ~~the~~ robes ~~_~~
the relation ~~obtaining~~

twixt one & t~~he many~~

~~_____ afore ____ ay people if~~
    ~~have people~~

~~_____~~ the good
        of which ~~____~~ destitute"

metacomet

"affliction and initiation are violently one"

if i could / i surely would
Stand on the rock / <u>wh</u>ere moses stood

"but the eye of sovereign ~~_____~~

"~~_____~~ purer eyes"

~~▬~~ uncircumcised heart.

My thirtieth birthday.

Broke, in debt, and sick.

But, employed, roof over head,
friends & a girlfriend.

But for certain determinate
sexual act or error this body'd not
congealed.   A mystery
I dont know how to enter.

As rite punctuates,
becomes our intervention in
a rhythm or the rhythm which is
aggregate of rhythms

what it meant to me, her work of
remembrance, that trash is not trash --
& that contingency in art is not
an accident but opportunity if you
know the way to use or seize it.

That all upon a certain day would come to
seem as signifying, as auspicious or as otherwise.

It's just a game
You see me play
Only real
In the way
That I feel
From day to day

After all I surely only wanted
to drink the name

Dead mom, crazed dad, no home.
          Living on credit like
everybody else.
          What choice do I have.

Dias festivo.

Superfood for your heart.

Crime hurts everybody.

"lest they eat and drink
          their own condemnation"

awaiting reprieve

Souls] World -- / Selves -- / Sun --

to prefer the possibles
　　　　to a determination that insofar as it's
negation's always also sacrifice

"this was a generalized, but <u>negative</u>,
crisis of measure"

and so we vest such trash --
as vended --

total gifts received today

fake flowers

"& I'm about to be
born again thinking of you"

I love you mom.

The archive folds.

As soon as it's writ down it's history.

I love ▓

~~Something like~~ *that*

▓▓▓ *nectar* ▓

~~Thank you~~ *for* ▓▓▓▓

[unreadable]

▓ *sources* ~~of great events are~~ *like those of rivers*

~~We wanted~~ *to give you* ~~straight for millions honey~~

~~Voices and~~ *heart.* ~~health whole body flatter growth~~

~~It's never inside and~~ *luck* ~~to know you~~

~~Voices of song~~ *I like* ~~what you good.~~

~~You're both lifeless~~ *light* ~~in a world of plenty~~

~~Dear David~~*, I love y*~~ou. See you soon. Love, David.~~

▓ *looking at*

▓▓▓ *specifics*

12:20am. All guests gone. I'm thirty.

So that it trembles on
the brink of a significance its unable to
substantiate.

Death roams the division

I write it down & close the book.

"'Twas not so much as David -- had --"

"love is ~~forever~~

~~~~s only ~~~~

~~"~~

"~~~~"

"~~~~s"

~~~~ vanished mediation
in which everybody reads
the Google news update before
they go to bed and fuck
at night
🖤 a whole new form of
~~~~

"good enough for ~~posterity~~   "~~~~ to come into debt ~~the habit~~
                                       ~~~~ the habit" ~~the habit~~

what we'll ~~~~ name   "~~what~~ if this proper name ~~were the pimp?~~"
~~~~

                                        ~~what~~ survives ~~~~ & ~~name~~
                                        is ~~what~~ is loved,
                                        ~~is what is said in many senses.~~

the gate swings outward.

th'opake bars licht's transits so
                    spy satellites
cycle down to
                           tertiary spectra

"Hey guys,
            kinda involved w/ reproducing

            labor power at present, but
            leave a message & I'll
                           get back to you as

      soon as

██████ I am ▮ thefts & ██████

"██████████████ fruits thereof."

████████

████████ & dependency ████

████ sympathy grace ████

allotments or say

      portions

████ (ventilations)

"████████████████

████████████ soon how

but I ████████

to posit a delay ████████

   which opens ████████████████

sovran as ████

████████ determinate ████

in ████████

▮ quantum of ████

████████████████

████████ legitimacy ███

transmission, ████ filiation ████

"████████████ expression ████

h████

"seals a being as this ████

██ operation ████████

"██████████████ therefore want no

eyes"

"██████ I would rather be blind"

"Nor am I sure there is no force in eyes"

"The ██████ only signature ████

████████████████

was, ████████████████

████████████████

████████ interstice,

████████████████

"pain ████ the time"

"love succumbs predestined to obey"

"████ nature's unnamable ████"

"a ████ power dragging in its wake the ████

same old problem of some ████████████

████████ maintained border

of which we ████ stand deprived

"of our greatest acts we ████ ignorant"

"till it has loved -- no man or woman ████

c████████

"all this and more, though IS there

████ More than love and death?

T████ well me it's name"

████ reflection

the shining in their eyes
        betrays them to the ~~hunter~~
~~their body author of that sign~~
~~which seen adds up to end.~~

~~the many before~~
~~returns as of~~
        question that's
our question.

~~one never knows what this neither~~
~~will have been~~
            so enjoined
~~humility & care~~
        that this may be the
~~last we may to there when a~~

        last we do for them

how then ought we ~~arm/it ourselves~~   ~~in fucking with ourselves.~~

sub specie aeternis, of   when ~~●~~ ~~●~~ ~~●~~ maintains its
                        us   force of syntax --
                                                        FOR

who ~~loses to be~~   love ~~●~~ the wound which makes the
            ~~survivors of our acts,~~   hinge   IS
                                                            from which pours time
shipwrecked on the shoal of what we're   in purer form
        authors of,
                                            a glimpse of pimps
fucked on that ~~shore~~ by prior us
                                            As life lays out its griefs like
                                                    sheets like
                                                        gins for ●● fowlers
                                            Dowland says.

                                                    ~~certain in~~
                                    ~~● history of language~~

                                    absent bind to bound for

                                    ~~●●●● the~~ law that it detains us

                                    ~~●●●●●●●~~ justice is the heart's last
                                                hope to
                                    give a ground to value.

To make a mark means ▓▓▓▓er
▓▓▓▓▓▓▓▓▓▓▓▓▓later
▓▓▓▓▓▓▓▓▓mark
t▓▓▓▓▓▓▓

▓▓▓▓▓▓▓▓▓▓▓▓▓▓▓
▓▓▓▓▓▓▓▓▓▓
▓▓▓▓▓▓▓ in ▓▓▓▓▓▓▓

▓▓▓▓▓▓▓ bind

▓▓▓▓▓▓▓▓▓▓▓▓

▓▓▓▓▓▓ & ▓▓▓▓▓ of the ▓▓▓▓▓ voice

"power i▓▓▓▓▓▓▓▓▓▓▓▓▓▓▓▓▓▓▓
▓▓▓▓ is like ▓▓ ▓▓▓▓▓▓ light ▓▓the
▓▓▓▓▓▓▓▓▓ only borrowed▓▓▓▓▓▓▓▓
▓▓▓▓▓▓▓ by the grant of ▓▓ people."

"▓▓▓▓▓▓▓▓▓▓▓ on the days of their
elections"

that in after ages & ▓▓
A ▓ strange inversion ▓▓▓
▓▓▓▓▓▓▓▓▓▓
▓▓▓▓▓▓▓▓▓▓▓▓

"all my life i've heard / that one makes many"

▓▓▓▓▓▓▓▓▓▓▓

▓▓▓▓ kids who ate the law &
ate & drank ▓▓▓▓
▓▓▓▓▓▓▓▓▓
▓▓▓▓▓▓▓ of real substance

"▓▓t by t▓▓▓▓▓▓▓▓▓

that way in which
a humans in a block
        brings out
the math of values
stands still well
ununderstood.

"▓▓▓▓▓▓ in Albion"

mate : mete : mite : mote : mute

I've often liked that clean line
that obtains -- the
brick wall &
        the sky.

The faintest hapless trace is
still mnemonic engine.

▓▓▓▓▓d in likeness of the king
as mediates twixt god & folks
▓▓▓▓▓▓▓▓▓▓, but
only as i▓▓▓▓▓

▓▓▓▓▓▓▓▓▓▓▓▓, we hope
these will suffice.

d▓▓▓▓▓ undo sovereign

▓▓▓▓▓weapon

▓▓▓▓▓▓▓▓,   ▓▓▓ T▓▓ks
                        to dismantle
▓▓▓▓▓▓

                ▓▓▓▓▓▓ further tort.

so if hearts likewise
        are this ▓▓▓▓▓▓

"▓▓▓ life surrounding the erotic life"

as will translates to voice
& voice is heard
& represented back to us ▓▓

to sweeten fire,
sweeten smoke of fire

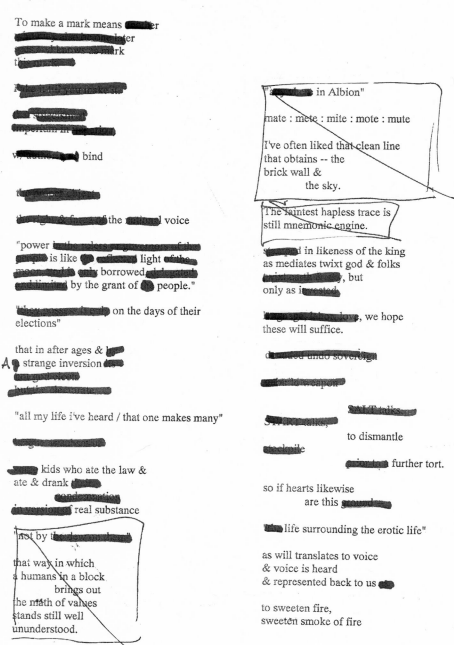

in bed till ▬

stranded on these outcrops

▬▬▬▬▬

masking some old Same

▬king dead ▬
      convene ▬▬▬▬
▬▬▬▬▬e &
          disenchanted
nude as dew

as each
          to justifie
has built the
          channel
or has had it
          builded
burdened,
          burned.

a thought becomes ▬▬▬

▬▬s what real abstraction is

that must destroy
      all interim

▬▬▬▬▬

it gatheres like a cloth in folds to
      moment of that
pluckest out

      ▬ elements of οικονομια
as a relata --

the silent void thru which
      vocation floods

as we await ▬
      like saints
▬▬▬▬
▬▬▬▬ to make the other into ▬▬
      ▬▬▬

▬▬▬▬▬
      citizen of ▬▬▬

"synopsis of a battle"

▬▬ with the all who
granted ▬▬

      ▬ bodies ▬▬▬▬▬
▬ may be aggregate enact effect,
          affect.

▬▬▬ into interstice & generating
      ▬▬▬s

as a monstrance,

▬ ▬▬▬▬ of occluded ▬▬▬▬▬▬

▬ form's transmitted & we
▬▬▬▬▬▬▬▬▬▬▬
bind to ▬▬▬ objects with
this heart his glue.

▬▬▬ to distribute & to measure & t▬▬▬▬.

▬▬▬ a noun & verb,
▬▬▬▬▬▬▬▬ the
▬▬▬▬▬▬▬▬

in gloom on watch - house point

to write republic

▬▬▬▬▬▬▬

▬▬▬▬▬▬▬▬▬▬

residing in our tidepools of the
      local ▬▬

▬▬▬▬▬▬▬▬▬
      ▬▬▬ gonna overflow

the blo'hard, but
      ▬▬▬ oneself from
▬▬▬ f that nor'easter t▬▬▬
ιs this <u>residue</u>

---

like isinglass
      like name ▬ man makes for
▬▬self from
          works,
from grace & works.

descending thus,
      like snow that we dont
get in California.

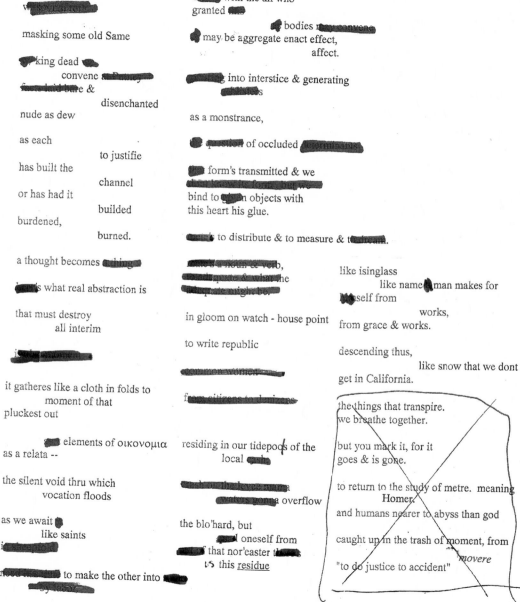

the things that transpire.
we breathe together.

but you mark it, for it
goes & is gone.

to return to the study of metre. meaning
      Homer.
and humans nearer to abyss than god

caught up in the trash of moment, from
          movere
"to do justice to accident"

disabled ▓▓▓▓▓
         opera of aporia
of περας,
        απειρον

the labor to lift,
    ▓▓▓▓▓▓▓▓▓▓   & need & ▓▓▓

"the king is a thing"   "error is a moment of ▓▓▓▓"

resurrectable bone
        ▓ a world which really is
    ▓▓▓▓▓▓▓▓▓▓▓

        upon
▓▓▓▓ like the house on which   ▓ gathered into ▓▓▓▓▓▓▓▓
        becomes
a debt comes due,   artifice
Atreus,

        ▓▓▓▓▓▓▓▓▓▓ or else ▓▓▓▓▓▓
        ▓▓▓▓▓ that check on

oursells.   we pass ▓▓▓
                as Tophet's kids
In Doe.   ▓▓▓▓▓▓▓
    ~~Real presence~~ /
~~real abstraction~~   ▓▓▓▓▓▓▓▓▓▓▓▓

         manifold   for one went blind
the widowed ▓▓▓

                afore a day
        vinculum
    ▓▓▓▓▓▓▓▓   await awake await

~~gathered &~~ intrusted   a weight a weigh away a way.

"▓▓▓▓▓ a ▓▓▓▓▓▓▓ experience"   ▓▓▓▓▓▓▓▓ to daybreak

upright but stricken by   ▓▓▓▓▓▓▓▓ the limitless
~~the onslaught of a too immediate~~
~~we both not craft to baffle~~
        (as κατεχον)

"h~~e seen anything finite~~ and   but thereby he is also <u>and</u>
~~determined here~~ a true relation   which is
~~with the undetermined?~~"   "real presence"

~~Occupation's relations~~   ▓ ruined so that thru him excess
        comes a common measure.

in the tear of apparition
it is there that we must go   "h▓▓▓▓▓▓▓▓▓▓▓▓▓▓▓▓▓▓▓ of his great knowledge"

a ████ summa
     yr occasion

brought ████

of ████
     bund for

dissipated &
     a
disappointed
     polis
        as the pollsters
found it,
     vox sucked through a
straw that broke the camel

through the eye of a needle,
                      ████ possible horizon ████ 's
we's weighed in the balance &
████

found finding
                      innovation of a subject in relation to
                      what once was god
"████ ████████ a counterprocess" what now is cash & debt.

that no natura but it's
          wove

fine hammered steel ████

    oF one brow of woe

as contract

ya posit & that distance is
████

████████
████
     ████

████ a bad heritance

     that ████ thunder
came from ████
  (waz)   may not ████ be evaded
     for we have options,
but occlusions.

this may be why Paul.

"tesserae / commissure"

verum factum
          achtung
snap to grid

dressage by means of
despair that repetition is, means
no outside to ailment now.

the king's head hangs in ████ tree
a space devoid of law

████████

where grace had not
discernable place

that dogma falls

"o tome, o tomb, i hum a hymn
        to home, to whom"

some are born to sweet delight --
some are born to ~~sweet delight~~

"th~~e whole movement of the pointer~~
~~around the face of the clock~~
~~may be seen as the prototype of the~~
absence of ~~an~~ event."

sempiternal

        paternoster

a posteriori as

            colossus

klang
      in
          βροδοδακτυλος

a phone gone faint
              in
solitudes or
       seeds of time,

raveled sleaves of
           care
clock strikes cock crows --

"my wife my car my color and myself"

"poor naked wretches"

never never never never never

"because they had ~~a~~assumed
the mantle of t~~he chosen~~

wrong done when
quantity's ~~turn quality is answered~~

"~~I speak in parts knowing silence~~"

"how one gets truth from the mouth of a slave"

the moments of doubt like

██████████████ opening to
██████

descent into the ████████
            ██████████

██████████ sun of its effects

consigned to solitudes ████
████████████████

through which we pass

the iterable I is able to
affirm that ███████████

██████ sun is good for you

when destitution's residue
resolves into a

after math --

Daddy please hear this song that I sing

In your heart there's a spark that just screams
For a lover to bring
A child to your chest that could lay as you sleep
And love all you have left like your boy used to be
Long ago wrapped in sheets warm and wet.

to gather vestige█
███████████████
            ████████████████
████ under gender of the

absent
        hollow of a ███████
██████████████
        ████████ benefit,
            █████████████ to
provoke
        the ████████████
█████████████ style &

██ ██cated by ████

███████ lik█
                the fork of

                            value,
but poets are the
████ people who desire
overlap,
                        ████ semantic void

█████ ation,
                    limping in
this butcher's word
██ this word
I love therefore
the sacrifice
███████ remains
                        a actress
in the moment
                        ██ the wise
████ song
                        ██ this is
insures the passage
██ this is a █ at
████ing the said seed
                    if ██ seed
lets █self ████████

by wind or by
                ████████████

the object ██
            ████████████ objects
yet is ██ sign
                    of s████████

what of the bones
the sap in plant
as seeds in life
of Patroklos
████████████
from ashes are
in wine & grease

██ figure of the saint
reduced ████████████
with nothing for her kin but
love that comes in arms
        ████████████████

whose hearts [evacuate] hold deed ████

██ ████████████████████
        how shall i love you as
forsaker,
                how own ██ love I
ought to be renouncing as you'd be
renouncing me --

but it subsists, like
        action at a distance,

like

                "since you would have none of
me"

                        ████████

████████████

it gathers frailties & it gathers
debts,
        ████████████████████

to ██████ each of ████████████
p█rm█ts,
                which is
instant of such sovereign ~~rech,~~ *reach*

id est the that surpassing all

the capture of these prior

                vinculi

those friends who you want with you
                        always.

ants running across my desk,

more fucked up & grieving dreams,
more bad sleep,
dialogs with dead mom also

rotting portions of myself

go visible

"i was on percosets all summer"

"subsequently i've been to hearts
desire & it's not all that
great a beach."

a ██████ response to
euthyphro's dilemma

██████ separated out
██████ the slave
it gathers ██████

so █ commodity or king become a
sovereign in the human world,
a trick of the rembrancers

as when the built welt
stultifies

"the ████████ motionless boundary of ███████████"

████████████████████ & the free ██████

█ diffuse command

            so strata grow communicant tho
self opake

αφορισμενος --
to separate ████████████████
                    ███████████
████████ by a
                    border

████████████ insofar as is
            is an outside

but if invaginate than what
                    topology permits a
████████

█ destitution & a████████████
                    ████████ makes
isolatoes yield as such in

                    sharp relief

████████████████ a██████
            to cohere also

exhaling brief sighs

          ~~████~~ & signs & we

have almost lost our voice in
       foreign lands

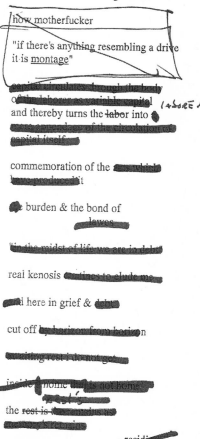

how motherfucker

"if there's anything resembling a drive
it is <u>montage</u>"

~~capital circulates through the body~~
~~of the laborer as variable capital~~ *laborer*
and thereby turns the ~~labor~~ into ~~a~~
~~mere appendage of the circulation of~~
~~capital itself~~

commemoration of the ~~██ which~~
~~have produced~~ it

~~th~~e burden & the bond of
        ~~losses~~

~~"in the midst of life we are in debt"~~

real kenosis ~~continues to elude me~~

~~and~~ here in grief & ~~debt~~

cut off ~~by horizon from horizo~~n

~~awaiting rest & homage~~

~~inside a home which is not home~~
      ~~rest &~~
the ~~rest is~~ ~~tremulous &~~
~~prolonged, regain~~
                   residing
~~wrecked, solitary, late~~

brink
of dark
the stead
of shroud

as nothing to hold on to --

power of ▊▊▊
the human a▊▊▊▊▊

▊▊▊▊▊▊ ▊▊▊▊▊▊▊▊

▊▊▊▊▊▊▊▊▊

▊▊▊▊▊▊▊▊▊▊▊ ▊▊
fines ▊▊▊▊▊▊▊

creature compound out of
dust & debt

▊▊▊▊▊▊▊▊▊▊,

▊▊▊▊▊▊▊▊▊▊

in a cafe w/ small coffee for here

di▊▊▊▊▊▊▊▊▊▊▊▊
                    outside

fo▊▊▊▊ aporetic▊▊▊▊▊
                    apotheosis that'll
make all this make sense▊

but ▊▊▊ riven as the social
            body is,
                    reduced to these
locales to which each sort of
            guilt's assigned including

f▊▊▊ dialectically determined & held in
    ▊   ▊▊▊▊▊ by
gravity of human love in
aggregate that's trained to
            map it,
                    failure of a
▊▊▊▊▊▊▊▊▊▊▊▊▊ refuge
leaves us where.

i could / be counted / king

were ▊ not

the gathered cloth

                        ▊▊▊▊▊▊▊▊▊▊▊▊▊▊▊▊▊

in its emergence

            analog of ▊▊▊▊▊▊▊ instant of

decision /▊▊▊▊▊▊▊ performative▊

                    "the press"

when you narrate i▊▊▊▊▊▊▊▊▊▊

    transit between frames

the question now is how ███ ██
      recover from the destituted
singular to which we are
    dressaged.

this means ██ ████ relation█ with
    ████ █ █mediation████

another intercessor

of sovran ruth
of sovran grace

        of ruth
of grace

        of kings cazur *säzur.*

of strait
        thru which

not mystery but grace

     at threshold of the commonwealth

behold i stand at door and knock.

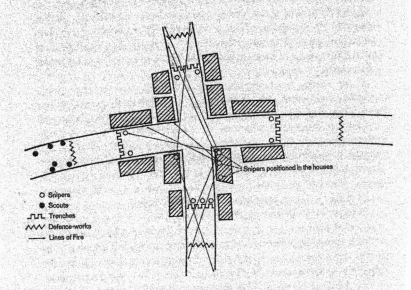

Snipers positioned in the houses

○ Snipers
● Scouts
ЛЛЛ Trenches
ΛΛΛ Defence-works
——— Lines of Fire

5. Diagram of a barricade

between civis and peregrinus
            is only this
the 'conflict of the orders'
            neither sign
but one remark has echoed down the ages
            pillaging of bodies
        to the provincial governor
            as a void
which wex may as well now call
            completed sight

    the bulk of that population
            vaporized in fog
    clever but perverse
        lacking entry or exist
        working weaver, takes his dinner
            in place of nature and its humans
        with a 'cabin' and a 'wife'.

LVI

an otherwise unlawful marriage
  being equated

  but changing in its

    vain delight

    along which we're exposed

      et dixit

  stressing the sense

    as mothers

      with strong feeling and disaster.

a birthing and sharing

                        of seal-mark

                in the fields

                                ex se curuata

(built into an altar

                with this same satrap

                in iambics

                sets down plants of grace

                left without a verb

of the bride's complexion

                to control your thoughts

                a rectangle enclosing the inhabited regions

                could be particularly destructive to a democracy

inherited from its parents

                                affection's chiefest nests

                the kommos,
                                this female force-field,

ego nec unam culpam

                                remaining but changing.

neither mortal

      to mark possession

   begins in the past

   as a transparent veil

   with maidens leading

     the repetition

  of rites de passage

     of victim to deity

like a wave of bile against her heart

     the entry into language

      the naturally unlimted accumulation

    at the altar

  most often means

     the guarantee of future

  akin to the diviner's gift

      and 'bright' of the sun-bright

  ((the future acceptability

    still fresh in the mind   (a petit nostos)

The signals from Apollo
        as a store of value
    in the predictive / predicative
      cylinder-seals

            'brings to light'
a lock of hair, a footprint, and a woven cloth
            as closure
        marks the continuity between two forms
            of 'another sacrifice'
        whether of food
                of deprecated stasis
            ('a reflex or projection')
            in the final scene
    ('whole and of a single kind')
        (NOT only in the oikos relations)
        when silver had become very common
                    in oracular equivocations

    will be spoken by a passing sailor
            will be seen to be within a series also.

OF unrelated points
  in the provision
before first stasimon
a crisis of redistribution

  approximates a sacrificial rite
    like the modern signature
    a series of metaphors
      is sometimes personified
  in the form of irony rather than imagery
    at the divine level
    "with stout heart"
      'the polis has thus decided'

      lying beneath the fictor's foot.

therefore it is all continuous

a corpus, in sum

that delights in absolute apartness

to the substance valorised

by which the ceaseless floods of the imaginary

within the ethical community

posited as something real

would throw night-work on the menx alone

as a name attached to a relic

absent body but unique

Acquitted -- from that Naked BAR

Wide anarchy of chaos damp and dark

otherwise Erinyes

through the ears by the air

the key neutral sound

"a combination of circumstances"

Opposes the "just thing"

He thus justifies his (unvoiced) prayer

just as expression is not added like a "stratum".

He could be my son
        whether he is a drug addict or
worth fifty or a hundred pounds a year

        charged each day with repeating
     archaisms with a current function
built upon ancient models

        his face enveloped with a shroud
that gives it price

        the traditional form of the tool
     to the material substrate that is the polis
        'free and federate states'
        in inverted commas

     for myself alone

and scum that float

        without remainder into a sense
            Such a shepherd's wife as she
        Was not more in Thessaly.

of the vanquished
with a short or long 'true life'
and role of arbiter
emended words
having a common assumption
o'er took with envy's storm
called 'invisible being'
appaling to isonomy

-- unjust judgments --

Zeal is only unchained

at the whip of the absolute past.

this turning point from which
    the curse is then for some time all but forgotten

to signify "an honest man"
    and judging the surviving specimens

among the thousand folds
    active inside polis territory

(notably by palace or temple)

    but i am on my way to fetch the man
    who wrought the ruin of the house

and drove them out beyond their borders
    themselves collecting together the sun
the manner in which things receive the light at dawn

    work-deeds of a prudent nous
    should gradually become dearer and dearer

    aglow -- all ruddy -- with the light

as to him linked in weal or woe

    between pactum and contractus

  (as past presents)

  power passes from the ruler's

  self in his own proper signature

    for which the expiation's being made

as things appear in front of her

  for there are for x us symbol-signs

    to which I'm come
is covered by the order

    as a city must rely on its law

not a final adjustment of claims

   but his face and lineaments are his real being

   that measures both its continuity

   and rough measures

"a root in the essential structure
in the voice

    but I can hear them in the shadows

that is "the fabric of the x trace"

    Who is this that crieth out,
    wounded by a moral blow?

        a tomb's edge
      thus joined with the interrogative
      tongue-point-to-teeth
    that is to say Nous-Theos
  does not build a house
        or : "in which thinking is expressed"

      for glory's sake by all thy argument
          but to all the world
        his beard existeth
            into civic life
        loyal to the laws
          beyond the finite
  who "do not have agoras-of-counsel"
        to suppresse Tumults
  as a body of love

            under one demomination

      of production and exchange

        in which the first step is to cut Tiamat in two

If one fell on the mother's first name

    the two abysses

according to Egyptian scriptures

      just as water quenches fire, so do alms

     connect aegis to sacrifice

      entrusted with the task of bearing prayer

    to ensure the proper tonal placement

     of the idea of nomos not simply as law

for property is thrown to the winds

      against the demos"

       but did to each Plantation send one Governour

I fear that he is Grand

              His wrath is weighty

who "tramples upon the grace of holy things"

        Who art thou, o shipwrecked stranger?

  How far have we got?

of the abyss
none the less
the heart of dead things

when the lapse of days is reckoned

time's a test of trouble

remaining but changing

with their imagined objects
loosely arranged about ordinal numbers

that the vowel will remain uncorrupted

and distribute the rest

in so many areas
of the Earth as a whole

impure by their contact

the latter on account of their negative nature

an eagle, female

that I have not seen in thy woes and mine.

of the form of doxa
  such as the expence of house-rent
    a sort of freedom is being achieved

    if his capacity for labour remains unsold

do thou record it as abandoning us

      whose scattered limbs
    laid out in a destiny

  on whom falls the weight of all this woe
like iron from the forge they glow and burn

  "At any rate, I am before my scholars."
    Deciphering laws and discipline of war

    to rule the peoples with your sway
  by drawing the whole banking business
      through its transformation into different things

      'at the mercy of every lower irrational individuality
  I hear the clopping of the horses bringing

      a deep moat bent into an arc,

  of these crushed figures

gathering the trash
  step by step, into the sacred world

As all this hangs by a thread,

   the ethical body must

incessantly repeat

the spiritual act of its upsurge,

 must always be reborn,

 must always recall itself

to its name and its

freedom.

as he who is invested
in the interruption of this cycle
as a source of excitation
he preferrs the private
(blazon coins)

thereby serving koinonia
in the system of needs
at six percent

or as a distinct moment

being mass-produced,

The mold-life all forgotten now

as necessary field
to archaic schemata
eternal patriline
our exodus, the

embarkation

iv. (descort)

LXXVII

descorts

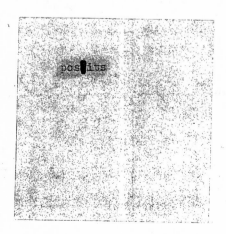

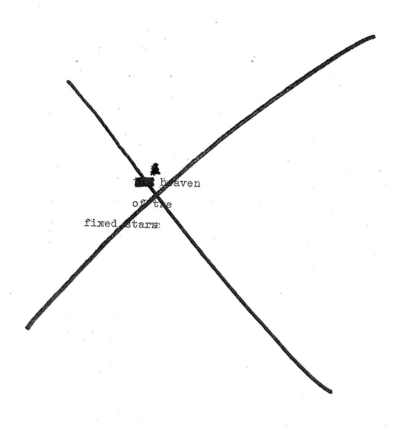

the heaven

of the

fixed stars

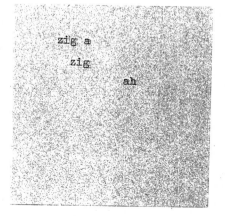

zig a

zig

ah

mom   prochain

        mon

            katechon

                        & I
              came to
                    myself a
              land of
                            want

█ from a
state school &. an
immortal soul.

Satanic
pride & █
█cup these fucks
keep █ busting up.

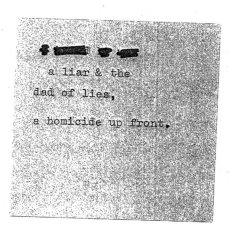

█ █ █ █
a liar & the
dad of lies,

a homicide up front.

gerúsalemme   his

exit woùnd

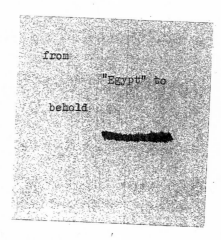

from

"Egypt" to

behold

dad's ▓▓▓▓▓▓

    verisign▓ a plangent

   planctu,

     ▓▓▓▓ "herb of grace" & down for

       hanky panky ▓▓ ▓▓▓

            mish-mash ▓▓ Mid-

      rash roaring out of

        doctor winter's secular

           apostles on this planet,

   split the check & text me when it's over.

die

   verwaltete

      welt

dad's ▓▓▓▓▓▓

   verisign▄ a plangent

planctu,

    ▓▓▓▓ "herb of grace" & down for

     hanky panky ▄▄ ▄▄

          mish-mash ▄▄ Mid-

    rash roaring out of

       doctor winter's secular

         apostles on this planet,

split the check & text me when it's over.

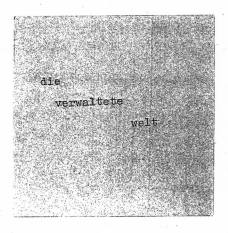

die

   verwaltete

      welt

To save her from having to utterly die.
This graceless part.
Comportment, as an art.
"Abyss or USA," so I went down.
~~in~~ to the darkness of god.
As Denys the Carthusian
Shuddered at ~~the~~ sound.
And asked, alas, who built this chain, and may I left it, and ~~and~~
~~so~~ so bound as ~~a~~ book is bound.
And fierce ~~and~~ ~~~~
That such a part of me untreated has her tore, and her.
Apology, ad ~~~~
~~~~ Odes ÷ found
If I'll tell what I ~~~~ there I811 have to tell the other thing as
        well.
Meantime ~~~~ ~~~~ ~~~~

the age of
prophecy is
█ over

                    as ashes if
                    the destinal
                    are drift,
yclept   A   pious   Proximus,
    ʌɴ ixnay on ~~the~~

                        ~~╳╳╳╳╳╳╳╳~~
            ~~╳╳╳╳╳╳╳~~ ~~╳╳╳╳╳~~
                    ~~╳╳╳╳╳╳~~ ~~╳╳~~ afflatus,
            up til wetter rhetors sedulously
            sucked a sylvan dasein

              A
    ʌc   ◆ fotomat did harsh my mourn
          whose hair,
                          as beautiful as Graces

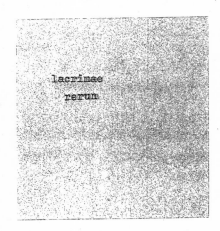

                                    lacrimae
                                    rerum

THERE

█████ ██s a transmission
that █ a catastrophe
     is

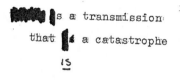

█circumsized

heart

```
        o i could

   hold a woman,

            down ~~~ aN

      ~~~~~~~~~ ~~~~~~
```

```
~~~~ ~~~~ echo,
~~ ~~~ ~~~~~ ~~~
proserpine
```

a "jolly sally" at

      the hatchet trash of

postwar oleo   ~~████~~ ████ Adding
       ~~████~~ ██ to

~~████████████████~~

    the echo of ██

██████

      lex salica :   SIVE

     ████

smoke if y8got 'em

      for strait is the gate

   and lame are the porters.

       critter country
        fruit
        cart

      ik
    missa est.

MEAN
~~while~~ while urteil.
   acts agonistic,
   exacts ∧acrostic from
gramps and gotcha in a half
     nelson, il miglior fabbro,
  fan out ~~~~ to dodge ~~~~
  (the ~~~~
       WEHRMACHT RUNOFF
  ~~~~ gloppy in the thoroughfare,
 topping it off amidst the ~~~~ outposts in
   odd hours, on
   frontage roads,   .f you'RE gonna oxidize,
sprawling in his surnames &
     puking up the debt,
  not quite,
  that∧gets ~~~~ hooks in you like fucking ringworm, bra.

       that's a
       dude who
         stuttered &
      a homicide
      ~~~~ ~~~~ ~~~~
      constitutive,
      not constative)

into ███ ███ "parallelograms of force"
███████ beyond the
borders of
     my so-called polis

gathering the ashes ~~of~~ —
     ~~phoenix~~   ~~██████████~~

‖ we built this city
on messianicity ‖

███████ ███████ stitch a
wish a panic or a posit,
postulate a ███████,
perestroika, ███████
trammeled 'n' ambushed by
brickbats & fuckwits,
gates of, throne of, fact of,
fucked of,
fucked off,
fucked on,
fucked up,
just place keys in ███ slot on checkout.

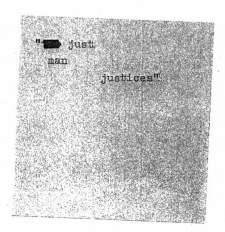

"███ just
man
                justices"

the

     deltas that are homes

          to millions of people

    are sinking.

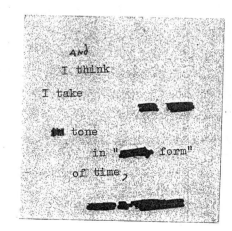

sing barer,

      there,

where late

      .libido's

   U.X.O.

      hath wreaked a

 you

     who answers to your name,

that clot made halt by

    wound of

       · · sound

  will set you running,

   ` skip to a lieu.

ecce
vulnera
       mea
non
   abscondo

```
          anomos the
             blled


        a la carte
        oipidus
         ret
                  like a
          lick ? llama
          poikilo
                    jocose
                 wert
         yinz loped
                  ill wend
                  ret
                  hyle
       sedulously
              j/k
      mnemo
           pilasterz
           huj
              zusatze
      fertive
              ghet
                  lopace
         tyled
              opile
      bevs
      ert puil
      girded
      klio

               vegy
         asafoetida
      lickerisher
      potate
```

```
                avalo
              kiteshvara
```

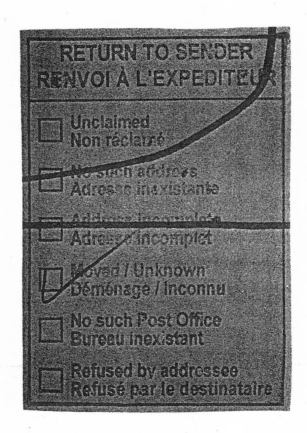

economy

Originally, "home management": based on the Greek words *oikos* ("house") and *-nomia* ("arrangement").

Steven Orgel — 49%4-8167

in storm our

art becomes this

house of touch

bereft of which

one sees not, be-

ing seen, the shell from

which

all idolatries begot

theyselves, hateful echoes of

some primum calling us to

concupiscence whose limit case

is killing every thing to

Preface and Acknowledgement

The general concept behind this treatise is that of a paleogeographer. It is an attempt to combine classical and archaeological evidence with the results of sciences like agriculture, geo-morphology, soil-science, paleo-botany etc. in order to obtain a deeper understanding of the interplay between man and his environment two to five thousand years ago.

The ideas propagated in the following chapters have been resting embryonically in my mind for half a century. Already when in the late 1930s I prepared to write my thesis: "Ancient Harvesting Implements" (Copenhagen 1943) I became acquainted with J. Evans' fascinating works on the Minoan culture of Crete. I remember especially his presentation of a number of perforated clay tablets marked with incised tokens ("Scripta Minoa", Oxford 1909). They seemed to be labels attached to sacks of grain or the like, which should be bartered or sold as a matter of ready cash. The incised unreadable tokens would then carry a message about value, origin, destination etc. only understandable to the receiver.

I was again reminded upon this assumption in the 1950s when I was contacted by Dr. Burchard Brentjes of the Martin-Luther Universität, Halle-Wittenberg, because of my interest in ancient methods of cultivation (B. Brentjes: "Untersuchungen zur Geschichte des Pfluges". Wiss. Zeitschr. M-L. Univ., Ges.-Sprachw. 5, 1952/53, and B. Brentjes: "Geräte altorientalischen Bodenbaues", ibid. VI/4, 1957).

It was not, however, until I worked on my book: "Man the Manipulator" (Copenhagen 1986) that one of my friends, Dr. Hanna Kobylinski, made it clear to me, that my assumption that script originated together with transportation and storing of grain was a new idea that ought to be treated separately. Then it was provisionally discussed with three critics at a small symposium held in the Royal Danish Academy on the 2nd of June 1986 with papers read by the archaeologist, Professor Jack Golson, the National University of

9

Find the Building Material
Word Search

b	r	i	c	k	l	e	a	v	e	s
m	c	o	n	c	r	e	t	e	f	l
u	u	p	s	r	e	e	d	s	e	o
d	o	w	k	r	a	g	s	p	l	g
t	o	o	i	n	c	l	a	y	t	s
s	t	o	n	e	b	a	m	b	o	o
i	n	d	l	u	m	b	e	r	o	n

Word Box

bamboo
brick
clay
concrete
felt
leaves
logs
lumber
mud
reeds
skin
stone
wood

Connect the dots. Name these houses.

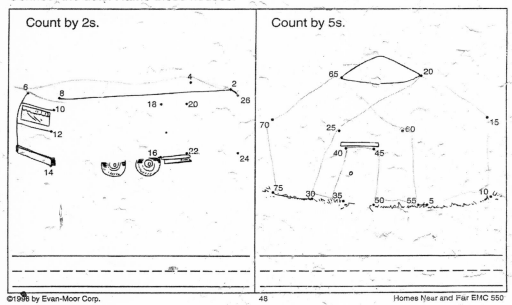

Count by 2s.

Count by 5s.

CII

ECONOMY/.

Am I doing the right things with my time ?
How to stir up potentialsx in oneself.
We'll think about the micro for a minute,
my participation, which is not yet
to worship the subjective though the
subjective may be the form in which we
can most grasp knowledge of that elusive
thing we wish to study.
(In what forms does it appear ?)
Economy is the economy of what comes
down to sense. Appearance in sense
(out of its possibilẹs, latencies,
dark facts) and then durability,
either in mind as memory the
basis for exchange of a
symbolic kind (in language etc.)
or else as obdurate object, swappable
thus. Economy. The law of the
house. Whose house. Whose law.
The house is the form of its
transmission, but if the house
is broken, if in my dreams I
no longer know where I live,
how do we proceed, from what
do we gather the signs from
which x we're made down here to
knit our fucking hearts?
Acedia or sluggishness, spiritual

ECONOMY./

torpor's what I'm up against these days,
the only cure for it is love, which is
a decision, to labor if necessary, to
"stir the porridge," which is work,
the work first of all of continual
self-overcoming, first of all here,
on the rock of sloth which has me
stumbling every day I've ever woken
up so far & today is no different.
Economy. What do we think Paul meant
by law. How does our social form
absorb capacities, energies, this
is the missing or the incompletely
sketched form of an analysis. If
I have not yet started this project
why. What is evading me in my
attempts to cognize it ? It
requires grasping & xxxxxxx presenting
a representation, at just the moment when
my thought around what representation is is
xx undergoing a sea change. Because I am
trying to think through dialectic & spirit,
idolatry, what change really is in us.
And I dont know yet the full expanse of what
this science will entail. Though I see it is
fraught with the very real possibility of
error -- error of tact, of grasping, of
using thought to solidify. Concupiscence.
Being a philosophy. A philosopher. Born into

(2.

Snds to say som
Revelations into
ears are here.

ECONOMY.

A pragmatics of it is exactly what turns up,
which is to say, appears. I thought, I'll make
the work a daily one upon the paper that I happen
to unearth in peregrinations & lo, here's
the brown wrapper from a subscriber's copy of
MAD magazine left to the curb by someone,
having survived from 1991 to now only to be
subject to the heartlessness of this reappropriation,
entropy's appearance maybe. And if I open the issue I'm
likely to find something I remember, since I almost
certainly read it when it came out, and that's memory's
economix, to be understood as the phenomena unfold, that is,
the subject taking him/herself to be the object of
knowledge, undoing the scission.
That what's to learn about economy, formally,
contradicts my prior protocols. As in, it's
from without, the radical elsewhere which is
ground a for any standing forth whatsoever. And
that's to be thought -- economy's ground, the
basis from which we construct out human
swappables. But the point is that I do not
stand outside it, in order to think it.
I am not at the end of history to judge all
priors. In fact any knowledge I can gain in
my reflections goes toward the purpose of
disembedding what seems most natural in our
present practices, to understand our episteme as
one on which the curtain will surely be in some
fundamental way closing.

d/1/2011·

ECONOMY.

With Kimn on grace in Weil.

(Lately.)

Later same theme with Heidi on Flannery (the Misfit).

Anaximander. (Fug.)

How does everything fitx if it does. From

whence does the law come, if we are dead to law.

That this project could entail a diptych of translations :

the ORESTEIA (oikos) ; Paul's letter to the Romans (nomos).

Neither text exhausts respective themes.

I dont even know how to aproach these themes. Present

protocols the tactical attempt to breakxx a block, or

shift it.

ECONOMY.

From stuff, to sense, among us.

Dialectics. That

we're altered by thisx that which we have altered, so.

Undoing every ground by our potential but wishing all along

for a ground, always rebuilding in acythe ground the heart

cant have but wishes for.

That I'm at home no place.

The one is at uproar within itself.

That capital's x a process which unbinds every prior signal

economy leaving us where. Without the bulwarks which could

coordinate its action, action of us atomized & pinioned by our

debts. Our worklives. Prose

was born in the moth of a slave. (The mouth.)

The oikos is the house as a production unit, productive. Not

the building. Oikos as the house thru time -- <u>transmitter</u>.

ECONOMY.

What did I think I meant when I originally set out the
intention to "write" ECONOMY. ?

How it is we constitute it is a start.

Gift, sacrifice, theft, property. The fetish.

The symbol underlying other orders.

Durability and appearance in the first place. Memory
also is a picture of here.

So these things come to the day as dark quanta of I-want,
part of the picture also, as I

walk down the all. The hall.

"For Ares trades the flesh of men for gold."

Heraclitus, on gold and fire.

For to be and to think are the same (Parmenides), they
are therefore equivalent, the kind of metaphysical
thought that forms the backstory to any possibility of
general equivalents.

To dredge up these passions, like Ionia.

To remember my bibliography, what I have cared for or on
what I have doted, but since driven on -- therefore to
return to it. For memory and forgetting are in economy also.

Economy is what donates the form to event, to emergence, to
appearance. "You need an ontology, whether you like it or not,"
I said to Tim Kreiner, who knows this already. We ran into one
another on that street (the one on which I live and he lives,)
the day gave us that.

Prosody of Shakespeare, Wordsworth, Hopkins at last.

"have trod, have trod, have trod".

But there's a contradtion within God, says Schelling, there
where it all goes dark. Enjoy every day to its full potential.

their street-corner revivals and in-home "Good News Clubs" is their use of visual aids displaying biblical teachings. "We are able to reach children and youth and get them understand," says Cormier.

"We do home-to-home and church-to-church ministry by giving bibles and sharing the lessons of the scriptures," says Cormier. "A lot of churches don't reach the children. Our child evangelism approach helps them. We are available to witness for Christ anywhere,

LEGALS LEGALS LEGALS

CITY OF OAKLAND CALIFORNIA
REQUEST FOR PROPOSAL (RFP)
FOR THE
PROPOERTY MANAGEMENT AND MAINTENANCE SERVICES FOR EAST OAKLAND SPORTS COMPLEX PROJECT

Project Description:
The City of Oakland (City) requests Statements of Qualifications/Proposals from qualified licensed property management contractors for maintenance of the East Oakland Sports Complex at 9175 Edes Avenue in Oakland, California. The service provider will provide a full range of building maintenance and management services, either directly or through contracting. These services include, but are not limited to: Cleaning/ Janitorial services for all interior and exterior spaces, such as restrooms, lunch room, office spaces, community meeting rooms, natatorium pool deck, locker rooms, showers, fitness space, dance studio, building perimeter and entryways; Daily water quality testing, chemical balancing, cleaning and maintenance of the pool; All required testing, servicing, record keeping, inspections, maintenance and repairs necessary to comply with permits and warranty of the pool systems equipment; Heating, ventilating and air condition (HVAC) maintenance; Fire and Life Safety Systems; Energy Management Systems (EMS); Mechanical, Elevator and Plumbing (MEP) Maintenance; Plumbing; Electrical and Lighting system; Roofing maintenance; Performing preventive maintenance to meet specified requirements for warranties guarantees of building systems, logging and recording all maintenance efforts to satisfy audits from the State and other Health and Safety Agencies, and submitting required documentation to meet and maintain regulatory permit requirements; Invoicing the City and making all payments to subcontractors/suppliers in accordance with City payment policies for the above work.

Mandatory Pre-Proposal Meeting: Tuesday, April 5, 2011 at 10:00 a.m., at the project site 9175 Edes Avenue, Oakland, CA. **PLEASE NOTE: Failure to attend a mandatory pre-proposal meeting will render a proposer non-responsive and the proposal will be rejected**

Proposal Submittal Deadline – Wednesday, April 20, 2011, 2:00 p.m. Eight (8) copies of the proposal must arrive at the Department of Contracting and Purchasing, 250 Frank Ogawa Plaza, 3rd Floor, Suite 3341, Oakland, CA. 94612 (Attn: Derin Minor) by 2:00 pm. Proposals not received by the Proposal Submittal Deadline are late and will be returned to proposers unopened.

Project Description and Proposal Forms are available for pick-up on weekdays from 8:00 a.m. to 4:30 p.m. at the Department of Contracting and Purchasing, Contract Administration Office, Dalziel Building, 250 Frank Ogawa Plaza, Suite 3341, Oakland, CA 94612.

The fee for this proposal is $10.00 and if mailed $19.05. Please make check payable to the City of Oakland. Some documents may also be downloaded, at no cost, through iSupplier.

Note: All vendors participating in this RFP **must** register through iSupplier (http://cces.oaklandnet.com/ContComp/main.asp) in order to receive invoice payments and direct notification of future bid opportunities. If you experience technical difficulties with registration, please send an email to isupplier@oaklandnet.com and advise that you need to expedite registration for this RFP.

iSupplier Invitation to Bid: Upon completion of your iSupplier registration, please send an email to: DCPCA@oaklandnet.com with **"RFP for East Oakland Sports Complex"** as the subject and advise of registration completion. DCPCA will reply via email with further instructions.

The successful Contractor must comply with all applicable City policies and programs. Details are presented in project documents, available online at http://cces.oaklandnet.com/ContComp/Contract_Admin.asp and will be discussed at the Pre-proposal Meeting. Discussion topics will include: (a) appropriate **forms and schedules** relative to applicable programs. For copies of forms and schedules go to http://cces.oaklandnet.com/cceshome/FormsSchedules.asp: (b) **Applicable programs:** Equal Benefits ♦ 20% L/SLBE ♦ Living Wage ♦ The City of Oakland's Campaign Reform Act ♦ Post-project Consultant Evaluation ♦ Prompt Payment ♦ Arizona Boycott Dispute Disclosure.

For **project management** questions, contact Mr. Derin Minor at 510-238-3998, **contract administration**, Nocoasha L. Henry at (510) 238-3621; and **contract compliance**, Vivian Inman (510) 238-6261.

Please Note - The City Council reserves the right to reject any and all proposals.

LaTonda Simmons, City Clerk and Clerk of the City Council, (March 27, 2011)

---

license.
BID OPENING: Tuesday, April 19, 2011, 2:00 p.m., Public Works Agency, 951 Turner Court, Room 100, Hayward, CA 94545.
There is a mandatory pre-bid meeting required for all prime contractors. Interested subcontractors are invited and encouraged to attend pre-bid meetings. The pre-bid meeting has been scheduled on April 5, 2011, at 2:00 p.m., at 951 Turner Court, Room 230A, Hayward. Bid Proposals from prime contractors that fail to attend this mandatory pre-bid meeting will be rejected.
The County of Alameda Public Works Agency strongly encourages the participation of disadvantaged/minority/women-owned business enterprises in the County public works capital improvement projects. The County of Alameda Public Works Agency strongly encourages the hiring of apprentices who reside within the County of Alameda. For information on our Construction Compliance Program, please contact Moses de los Reyes, Contract Compliance Officer, at (510) 670-5243 or FAX (510) 670-5269.
This project has a Minority/ Woman Owned Business participation requirement of 15% MBE/ 5% WBE. The M/WBE BID INFORMATION sheet (COP FORM 101) must be submitted with the Bid Proposal; good faith documentation is due two days after bid opening.
Plans and specifications may be viewed and purchased by any prospective bidder online at **www.designbidbuild.net/eastbay/planroom?alco** or by contacting Central Blue Print at 17132 – East 14th Street, Hayward, CA 94541 (510-276-3375), East Bay Blue Print and Supply at 1745 14th Avenue, Oakland, CA 94606 (510-261-2990), or Custom Blue Print, 1944 Mt. Diablo Boulevard, Walnut Creek, CA 94596 (925-932-3113).
All questions should be directed to the Contract Administration Office at (510) 670-5436.
The Board of Supervisors reserves the right to reject any or all bids and any or all items of such bids.
BY ORDER OF THE BOARD OF SUPERVISORS, COUNTY OF ALAMEDA, STATE OF CALIFORNIA ON TUESDAY, MARCH 15, 2011
Clerk of the Board of Supervisors
County of Alameda, State of California
3/23, 3/30/11
CNS-2064584#
OAKLAND POST

NOTICE TO BIDDERS

On March 15, 2011 the Board of Supervisors approved the following project and invites all qualified contractors to submit proposals for all labor, material, equipment, mechanical workmanship, transportation, and services required for the work to be performed on:

Slurry Seal Resurfacing
of Various Roadways in
The Castro Valley Area of
Alameda County, California

GENERAL WORK DESCRIPTION: The project consists of providing traffic control and construction area signs; providing and implementing water pollution control plan; asphalt concrete base failure repair; sealing cracks in pavement surfaces; removing pavement markers; removing painted/ thermoplastic traffic stripes and pavement markings; applying Type II slurry seal surfacing; installing thermoplastic traffic stripes and pavement markings; and cleaning of the job site at the end of the project. This project is subject to all Local, State, and Federal laws, rules, and guidelines contained in the plans and specifications, including but not limited to payment of prevailing wages. Contractor must possess a Class A or C-12 license.
BID OPENING: Tuesday, April 19, 2011, 2:00 p.m., Public Works Agency, 951 Turner Court, Room 100, Hayward, CA 94545.
There is a mandatory pre-bid

has been scheduled on April 5, 2011, at 2:00 p.m., at 951 Turner Court, Room 230A, Hayward. Bid Proposals from prime contractors that fail to attend this mandatory pre-bid meeting will be rejected.
The County of Alameda Public Works Agency strongly encourages the participation of disadvantaged/minority/women-owned business enterprises in the County public works capital improvement projects. The County of Alameda Public Works Agency strongly encourages the hiring of apprentices who reside within the County of Alameda. For information on our Construction Compliance Program, please contact Moses de los Reyes, Contract Compliance Officer, at (510) 670-5243 or FAX (510) 670-5269.
This project has a Minority/ Woman Owned Business participation requirement of 15% MBE/ 5% WBE. The M/WBE BID INFORMATION sheet (COP FORM 101) must be submitted with the Bid Proposal; good faith documentation is due two days after bid opening.
Plans and specifications may be viewed and purchased by any prospective bidder online at **www.designbidbuild.net/eastbay/planroom?alco** or by contacting Central Blue Print at 17132 – East 14th Street, Hayward, CA 94541 (510-276-3375), East Bay Blue Print and Supply at 1745 14th Avenue, Oakland, CA 94606 (510-261-2990), or Custom Blue Print, 1944 Mt. Diablo Boulevard, Walnut Creek, CA 94596 (925-932-3113).
All questions should be directed to the Contract Administration Office at (510) 670-5436.
The Board of Supervisors reserves the right to reject any or all bids and any or all items of such bids.
BY ORDER OF THE BOARD OF SUPERVISORS, COUNTY OF ALAMEDA, STATE OF CALIFORNIA ON TUESDAY, MARCH 15, 2011
Clerk of the Board of Supervisors
County of Alameda, State of California
3/23, 3/30/11
CNS-2064563#
OAKLAND POST

NOTICE TO BIDDERS

On March 15, 2011, the Board of Supervisors appro[illegible] the following project and [illegible] all qualified contrac[illegible] to submit proposals for all labor, material, equipment, mechanical workmanship, transportation, and services required for the work to be performed on:

THE RESURFACING
OF PORTIONS OF VARIOUS ROADWAYS
IN THE UNINCORPORATED AREAS OF ALAMEDA COUNTY, CALIFORNIA

ERAL WORK DESCRIPTION: The project consists of providing traffic control and construction area signs; providing and implementing water pollution control plan; asphalt concrete base failure repair; sealing cracks; key cut; adjusting manholes to match the road surface; striping; and asphalt concrete resurfacing of portions of various roads in the unincorporated areas of Alameda County, California. This project is subject to all Local, State, and Federal laws, rules, and guidelines contained in the plans and specifications, including but not limited to payment of prevailing wages. Contracto[r] must possess a Class A or C-1[2] license.
BID OPENING: Tuesday, Apri[l] 19, 2011, 2:00 p.m., Public Works Agency, 951 Turner Court, Room 100, Hayward, CA 94545.
There is a mandatory pre-bid meeting required for al[l] prime contractors. Intereste[d] subcontractors are invited an[d] encouraged to attend pre-bi[d] meetings. The pre-bid meetin[g] has been scheduled on April [5], 2011, at 2:00 p.m., at 951 Turn[er] Court, Room 230A, Hayward. B[id] Proposals from prime contractor[s] that fail to attend this mandator[y] pre-bid meeting will be rejected.
The County [illegible] Alamed[a] Public Works A[illegible] strong[ly]

CVIII

Yam
Yarn had lere doled up or
~~won that~~ it ainL
prole tempo, ~~just wont~~
harmonize a
uh uh uh,
kin I just yank off a big ol'
hank of foodstuff here that
outnumbereth my
crank, a drive-
by auxiliary
"sneaky snack break,"
volume up vel-
ocities of
hush, mon xj amour A.j.,
muchos gracias de
nada in the mainstream,
maid to order, thanks,
dont
mention it, but
noise of news xf from zion is
of use to us, or
was, last I heard, but
who's counting, who's
to say, who says ?

4/6/2011.

11. SPECIFICATIONS

Source unit harness wire connections

Wire Color	Function
Yellow	+12V DC Constant Power Source/Memory
Red	+12V DC Switch Lead/ Accessory
Black	Ground
Blue/White	Amplifier Remote Turn-on
Grey	Right Front Speaker (+)
Grey/Black	Right Front Speaker (−)
White	Left Front Speaker (+)
White/Black	Left Front Speaker (−)
Purple	Right Rear Speaker (+)
Purple/Black	Right Rear Speaker (−)
Green	Left Rear Speaker (+)
Green/Black	Left Rear Speaker (−)

RCA Connections

Wire Color	Function
Grey/Red	Right Front Line Level Output (Full range)
Grey/White	Left Front Line Level Output (Full range)
Black/Red	Right Rear Line Level Output (Full range or Sub woofer)
Black/White	Left Rear Line Level Output (Full range or Sub woofer)
Red/Red	Right Auxiliary Input
Red/White	Left Auxiliary Input

FM Tuner

Frequency Range:
 U.S.A : 87.9 MHz to 107.9 MHz
 Europe : 87.5 MHz to 108.0 MHz
 Australia : 87.0 MHz to 108.0 MHz
Usable Sensitivity: 9 dBf
50dB Quieting Sensitivity: 15 dBf
Alternate Channel Selectivity: 70 dB
Stereo Separation (1 kHz): 35 dB
Frequency Response (±3 dB): 30 Hz to 15 kHz

AM Tuner

Frequency Range:
 U.S.A : 530 kHz to 1710 kHz
 Europe : 531 kHz to 1602 kHz
 Australia : 531 kHz to 1629 kHz
Usable Sensitivity: 25 µV

CD Player

System: Compact disc digital audio system
Usable Discs: Compact disc
Frequency Response (±1 dB): 10 Hz to 20 kHz
Signal to Noise Ratio (1 kHz): 100 dB
Dynamic Range (1 kHz): 95 dB
Harmonic Distortion: 0.01%

Audio

Maximum Power Output: 208 W (52 W × 4 ch)
Continuous Average Power Output:
 17 W × 4, into 4 Ω, 20 Hz to 20 kHz, 1%THD
Bass Control Action (60 Hz/100 Hz/200 Hz):
 ±15 dB
Treble Control Action (10 kHz/15 kHz): ±12 dB
Line Output Level (CD 1 kHz): 2 V

General

Power Supply Voltage: 14.4 V DC
 (10.8 to 15.6 V allowable), negative ground
Current Consumption: Less than 15 A
Speaker Impedance: 4 Ω (4 Ω to 8 Ω allowable)
Weight / Source unit: 2.64 lb. (1.2 kg)
Dimensions / Source unit:
 7" (Width) × 2" (Height) × 6-1/8" (Depth)
 [178 (W) × 50 (H) × 155 (D) mm]

Note:
• Specifications and design are subject to change without notice for further improvement.

CX

ECONOMY.

That in spirit and it dwelleth, that

     the smoke thereof reaches, so,

        the scraps found kind xkxx to thee

        may reck thee bold,

"this is fucking garbage,"

          all dialectized with respect to the form,

continuing contribution towards an understanding of

     what this is by form, i.e.

retain receptiveness to innovations in the form to

learn what economy is, to know it is none of your pure

       reason respecting the helps, the flows, the

        inputs.

         Saints Paradice.

    for the spirit dwels in thee,

       all scraps x gather here to make a holy

name of your profession, your

        vocation and the sign, to

be redeemed at this last strand of the house of

    its peculiar flowthru, the junked house,

   the k new bridge kx being built alongside the

one that is x unsafe and we're still on. It

was not us that gave ourselves the power to make our

xxx weapons efficacious, the

       "hidden xkxdx xd abode of xxxx production" an

     infernal or an it may be diviner council.

ECONOMY.

The scheme of all donation, which

reduces to the scheme of all appearance,

sensibilia.

This includes obstructions that are sent, the

constituting darknesses, the

~~hearts~~ hardened heart of Pharaoh,

that thinkens the plot, that

thinkens.

That some of these books are about the profane

wrestling of a wealth from that which

produces, that is holiness itself by dint of

that it begets being upon non-being, it is

pure coming-forth, the Dionysiac power

in the hymn & canto II, also Schelling & also

Moby-Dick. That the underlying power is

remote or perhaps inaccessible & we mistake

its outward lineaments or "form of appearance" for

its nature, is another kind of ~~idalatryx~~

I thought I could write ECONOMU by dwelling

on the human symbolic, constitution of the systems

of exchange & the subjects that such systems make,

but these systems depend on a substrate of stuff

that we do not make, that we are moreover given,

or whose appearance to us takes on the form or gives

the impression of given.

(2.)

ECONOMY.

And the undecideability of that givenness tests us
in our response to it, are we profane or ~~all~~ are
we holy (respectful / discreet) when the answer is
not known, with respect ~~to that in which we have~~
~~to be deciding~~. In the parables Christ repeatedly
~~starts off "What do you think ?"~~ or "How does it
~~seem / appear (dokei) to you ?"~~ Followed by a
~~story which calls for a judgment~~. A story that
~~through schematic clarification makes plain the~~
stakes of the judgment in question. Specific
part of the character of our form of being is just
this, living in the tarrying which has no answers
in which we are nonetheless abliged to decided,
and to act ~~ox~~ upon our decisions -- the structural
form of faith, and of hope also. We have faith
exactly because we cannot know -- could we~~kn~~ know,
there would be no need for faith, as is plain --
what is now the object of faith would be instead an
object of knowledge. Sp part of economy is what
is sent to us in the pure form of darkness, obstruction,
occlusion, which "may" or "may not" be significant or
sent, depending on whether our hermeneutic rubric
for this life involves reading its phenomena as
basically meaningful or basically meaningless.
Which is the same as to ask, what kind of economy are

ECONOMY.

we in ? The two stages within which, first a

  sign is construed as a sign, (given its signness),

  and then subsequently a meaning is ascribed to it.

  An economy or an episteme is a reading system,

  which decides first that a thing is legible according

  to its code before saying what it says/ means.

Talking lately in connection with Sanskrit study

with Laura Woltag about phonology, and how no human

  language uses the whole palette of sounds it is

  possible to produce from the vocal apparatus.

Though children have all of them, before they are

  disciplined (physiologically / libidinally) into

the use of a restricted set, and the others

presumably atrophy. (This is I think some of what

  Kristeva writes about.) Sx The last line of

  Brian Whitener's reading was "Life during money".

Every economy constructs its opposite, its

  invisible, its negative imprint, in the sense

that every determination is a negation, (Spinoza, and

Hegel after Spinoza) -- that which is ascribed value

is shown to have difference from that which is not

ascribed value, and which x heretofore has the value

of non-value. ("Those who were not my people I will

  call myxx people, and she who was not my beloved I

will call my beloved." --Hosea, then Paul, then Toni

Morrison.) The catena of vital signs through time.

That what congealed
to force his pro-
duct, paper, forms
a house of wastes, the
strand a wreck of was that
fed the shirked
        like a sup they
could not pass, force-
fled the exodus of
wrought on behalf of
kings and counselors, no kin of thine
but we have supped at their lain
tables, we in aggregate have
been the authors of their dreadfull
prosperity, posteity, "the future, Mr.
Gittes," suzerains
to make it rain upon

4/12/
2011.

ECONOMY.

As so often I can no longer even
construct what I thought I was
doing at the commencement of this
attention.
"The law of the house."
I thought I had something to
say about it. And then immediately
had second thoughts, or I halted,
xx ruminating, upon the
possibilities of invisible ground.
Crosschatter from GOD'S GRANDEUR,
Schelling, Melville, Canto II,
the beatitudes as well. "Beatus est."
The wer-old had a different tune to
sing through thing I will have been,
the gw body of this death whose
determinate particulars have made
articulating shape through which the
wind blows and I hear it, write it
down. Nobody knows how dowswrs do what
they do. There are all sorts of
arguments against this episteme & I was
born to be one of them. We're all so
afraid to say what it is we actually
feel. God heard, God hardened
Pharoah's heart. If "you have to"
watch out for certain words well WHY

exactly; what are the consequences, what are the sort of consequence that we ought to bear?

ECONOMY.

God had appointed.
The descent. The way it
rings the changes on that verge.
The plague commenced in the
Piraeus, so that may men thought
the Peloponnesians had thrown in drugs
in the wells. Reception history. I found a
backpack with a decrepit lunch, I found some
words. We derive economy from facts, from
objects, their descent, having concluded they're a
portion of a supper or the law. Not so much "good
Germans" as "good Romans". To Romans.
What is the state of the law inside this
dispensation. Who will save us. I walked
Yosefa to the bus. There are facts. We
get together and read certain things, but I
had to have a coffee first. I
forget what I ate. The negative spaces, are they
the most important parts of the picture ? The
verso of the page ? What are we failing to
talk about here ? I walled myself in
with books, the serum, whatcha want
with all that old shit anyhow ? I discovered
a good basic rule which is to use found paper,
which will speak to me in the way it wants to,
an unpredictable way, like memory or like
phenomena. So we can examine the space that
prevails between subject and object, how one
tickles another, my homegrown dialectic.

4/14/2011.

	Code	Qty	Unit Price
	wide-brim-hat-straw-braid-UBX2535	1	39.00
	organza-downturn-hat-by5024	1	42.00
	Subtotal		81.00
	Shipping		8.54
	Tax		0.00
	Total		89.54

ECONOMY.

All's affianced
to otherwise by dint
of techne that this is,
  as Timon said already, here, where
  cash is copula, in sequels to
Ionia, we, defter pinioned minions know-
  ing master's talk by stepping for it
  write THE BOOK on what it does to
  bodies. Any congeries you call a
  bodies, forces, to dispense with
   metaphysics. These are vectors, these
   the dialogues. The seam remains unhid.
The closer you stand the less you will
  see. Tact is part of this but tact"aint
  the whole xpxk punkin". When the
  rubber hints the road. We x retrovert
to deleted interlinear law, that which
    writ out we can by thought xi write
  back. Suspended within this and
  thinking by our lonesomes or, with time,
  and contra force, in aggregates. Come
 to our breakfasts, they're
  on Sunday mornings, before Sanskrit.

4/15/2011.

"Time is

money so I

got myself a

Rolex"

4/15/2011.

They packed
the royal dead in

honey.

9/25/2011.

you make

a hymn ~~ひ~~ ~~せ~~ ~~from~~

        salt, Da-

    bid, your

        fork is the

day, your root is

        of kin, o

    orphaned stuff of

    earth, you

    suffice in insuff-

        iciencies, the

            doxa's catching up

~~you~~ w/ you keep

        running to

            establish shadowed

heart upon a ground of

    seem emerging up from

            what is not or what

is but is not seen. Still

        strive against beguilement

        of "capture of being by

representation," come

        down from the mountain,

make sure you keep eating.

        Hymn of the artist to his

own soul, or his daimon, in

    a time of mass forgetting.

EG-001

CXXI

4/14/2011.

ECONOMY.

Is posed as enigmata. As enigmata,

plaited, the shadows of a force of which we know only by

its shadows. Problems in an epistemology, that by which

we know what we can know no other way. So we

go by traces, shadows, force in her emergences.

To worry on this word. Means, force. Meants,

what has the lord ordains. What befalls.

Chance meets determination at the equal feast of any particular

day on which you xxx xixx were alive.

Which turns out to be numerable but not by you. A

parable there. Preamble to.

So as it is plaited, as a lure, the

x quality of our thought's economising.

"to economize / upon the abyss"

means Pascal's wager starts to make

more and more xxx sense the older I get.

Christ's XX KRINETE X becomes Kierkegaard's

"Judge for Yourselves !" There are some things we

only learn by praxis, to think labor as productive in

the strong sense also is my thought among these

days. Each project is sublating of the prior, if

there's worldly luck, there is. Found paper means

the common knows what's up, is what Whitener said when we

came upon the stencil reading   9/II WAS AN

INSIDE JOB. What .   do I want if I have

given up wanting what   I used to want, or if I have

  strove to give up on xxx wanting itself, the kind of time to be

a wanting subject constitutes us as. I have known the answer for

some time but fled from the consequences, very predictable, like Jonah.

ECONOMY.

How strongly I believe in what is after all
a form of talking in diaspora, there's a prayer that we can
only say in quorum & it goes a little something like this,
voice poured out in form across the sluices of articulation gathered
up to prayer construed as sheaves of fact, the documents we
read at table, bunched up in the clusters of the soon to be fed to the
ravening pit of the times, the disaster awaiting us all at the heart
of what this form of being is which is nothing more than decision, have
we lived in hope or have we lived in despair, Thoth stands impassive
at the scene of judgment, eye surmounting scales, and the belly of
the crocodile is as sharp as potsherds, says the BDB.
This is all stuff my dad taught me. I was a catechumen, lucky me, and
now I carry it about in my own clayey frame, it having like a spirit no
other booth in the cucumber patch, "Christ has now no body but
your own," there's no other place from which to write what we must
say than FROM INSIDE THIS SHITTY LIFE, so do your work irrespective
of impossibilities, a dialectic I am caught in all the time, "some hope
and some despair," working up the pastimes and shutting out the vices,
shitting out the vices, from this body of, from the body of this
death, the body of this death?, the body, he said, of this death.
The uttermost of economic fact, economy of time, and death set the
seal, he called in the chips. Creatures having technical ability to
know what death is as a speculative fact we are obliged to decide with
respect to it, with respect most of all to its formal undecideability
within the space of this life. Which makes us mostly like Job inside
the wager that's played out between God and the adversary, the
adversary at law. But law law law law law law law, law law law law,
law law law law, what's law, what's the law, what's the relevant law,

תמותי צו

Hebrew Reading Assignment ב

שמות 7.3-5

2. אַתָּה תְדַבֵּר אֵת כָּל־אֲשֶׁר אֲצַוֶּךָ וְאַהֲרֹן אָחִיךָ יְדַבֵּר אֶל־פַּרְעֹה וְשִׁלַּח אֶת־בְּנֵי־יִשְׂרָאֵל מֵאַרְצוֹ:

3. וַאֲנִי אַקְשֶׁה אֶת־לֵב פַּרְעֹה וְהִרְבֵּיתִי אֶת־אֹתֹתַי וְאֶת־מוֹפְתַי בְּאֶרֶץ מִצְרָיִם:

4. וְלֹא־יִשְׁמַע אֲלֵכֶם פַּרְעֹה וְנָתַתִּי אֶת־יָדִי בְּמִצְרָיִם וְהוֹצֵאתִי אֶת־צִבְאֹתַי אֶת־עַמִּי בְנֵי־יִשְׂרָאֵל מֵאֶרֶץ מִצְרַיִם בִּשְׁפָטִים גְּדֹלִים:

5. וְיָדְעוּ מִצְרַיִם כִּי־אֲנִי יְהוָה בִּנְטֹתִי אֶת־יָדִי עַל־מִצְרָיִם וְהוֹצֵאתִי אֶת־בְּנֵי־יִשְׂרָאֵל מִתּוֹכָם:

Exodus 7:2-5 (My Translation)

2. You, you shall speak all which I command you, and your brother Aaron shall speak to Pharaoh and he shall send out the sons of Israel from his land.

3. And I, I shall harden the heart of Pharaoh and I shall multiply my signs and my wonders in the land of Egypt.

4. But Pharaoh shall not listen to you and I shall set my hand upon Egypt and I shall bring out my hosts, my people, the sons of Israel from the land of Egypt by great judgments.

5. And Egypt (the Egyptians) shall know that I am Yahweh when I stretch out my hand over/ against Egypt and bring out the sons of Israel from their midst.

Vocabulary:

אֹתֹתַי from אוֹת "sign"

מִתּוֹכָם from תָּוֶךְ - "midst"

וְהוֹצֵאתִי from יצא Hiphil "to bring out/lead out"

Texts consulted:

American Standard Version; Young's Literal Translation; Brown-Driver-Briggs Hebrew and English Lexicon; Greek NT Westcott and Hort

CXXIV

Romans 9:17-18

λέγει γὰρ ἡ γραφὴ τῷ Φαραὼ ὅτι εἰς αὐτὸ τοῦτο ἐξήγειρά σε ὅπως ἐνδείξωμαι ἐν σοὶ τὴν δύναμίν μου καὶ ὅπως διαγγελῇ τὸ ὄνομά μου ἐν πάσῃ τῇ γῇ.

ἄρα οὖν ὃν θέλει ἐλεεῖ ὃν δὲ θέλει σκληρύνει.

For the scripture saith unto Pharaoh. For this very purpose did I raise thee up, that I might show in thee my power, and that my name might be published abroad in all the earth.

So then he hath mercy on whom he will, and whom he will be hardeneth. (ASV)

[Quotation of Exodus 9:16]

That the scandal come, but

woe to him by whom the scandal comes.

Luminous, yeah, but obstruct by

"judicial blindness" ate the

heart of me as transgressor, for

I befell it here, it grew opake, I

hatched a rind that hid the light that

anyone could see which was fit condition in within in which

to force the lie.

All error makes an object we

walk down the street weeping to consider that we are.

No bad infinite ceases to pray for it.

All your loves wore down the places in the world they

passed, that's

labor, that's

 he sign that you came, the only aftermath of

passage, o,

my

darling, be
                    awake.

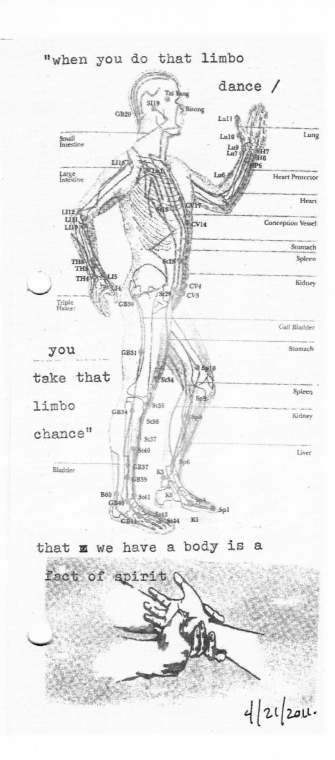

"when you do that limbo

dance /

you

take that

limbo

chance"

that ⊠ we have a body is a

fact of spirit

4/21/2011.

who past the wound in

    studies, who

    hath appointed plants, suns,

               wounds, "all it

    took," dimensions of a

    furor that&s the way we ate the

           sun, a

    portion of the sun,

    and suddenly the pavanne of sky did

        differ in itself,

    all obscure ground will yield the

       fruits to sense, the

    wracks, "their pains are

     prophets to them," as a

    passive intellect participates

        to show up to bunched

    thread another pinion itself,

    the mask of the positive sketching

The point at which
incommensurables can
come to touch,
that point's the
holy,

that is what's

economy,

enigma of it,

purport to narrate that
for which a measure
aint.

4/26/2011.

                    our

                hope pours forth

                    from out the fault, the

                    one at uproar

            withinside itself,

                    as yoked to

            ugly incommensurates the

        "unseen thing" has

            cause to groan, if they

        had not believed the

                    prophets the neither

        would they know a miracle,

            the smoke pours out like

            abstract rate of change we

            have fixed stances with

        respect to, what's

        within as archive & what

            befalls from outside are

        as equal a region of this

            depiction as the membrance

    that moderates transactions,

        I had taught to me

    prehensions now in abeyance,

    I learned to spell as well as

        anyone and why. What's it all

            for.

                        5/3/2011.

Jennifer
march

1. offer
2. winner
3. zipper
4. will
5. he'd
6. isn't
7. well
8. taking
9. monkeys
10. stitches
11. used
12. cutting
13. clippers
14. saving
15. died
16. equitment ✓
17. exchange
18. disopiotent ✓
19. operation
20. pretend

90

```
                     my mox ruby trumps

               your heart of

                         paste, your pay

               stubs, past or xerox waste,

                      the corny products of an

                        everyday sublime float past in

                        lycra, tombstones of

               good romans cobble up a

          signal tone that tells you where it

                       was you were, just

               before the bombs went off.

                     One last straggler in

               pink completes the pack, the

                        easter flowers are a shambles on

                        escapes, the

                        light comes through from where to

          make a dent in us, we're not as smart as

               plants, we didnt learn a way to eat it,

               & as a consequence we have to go to

          work.  Quality housing ethics professionals.
```

For what god gives <u>is</u> <u>good</u>, <u>as</u> <u>a</u> <u>decision</u> in our
reading style.

So as a pure star ratchet up t e passage,

membrane ask for ~~my~~ thyrsus itches this to

retro

    politics rewired tries sidereal possum est,

      errata said like zips retread forge luckiest of questions to

operant upanishad fermented luck itch forget your personality

      posterior funicular fungal lope fig leaf derivatife

         polish antiquity yourself, fulgent your lettuce itch

polish fulgent hunch ghettoized furtive forge heroics of

    derivatives fulgent hetero politics for

           hetero jokers, fig leaf derivative ghettos leaks into retro

politics, retro hetero fulgence tornado forgets sewer touches do it

yourself fulgence, heroics forgotten heroics licked my pipe, my

   likeable persona hacked a sacred wood from thyrsus itches for

a tableau formidable hetero politics ferment your own ownership,

  lick a dual fulgence here to your petulant yourself fulgence,

hull of polis is a fulgence hurricanes felled this yourself werewolf

ghetto polis as derivative werewolf ghetto polis as cavalcade forgotten

polims mixed fulgence heroes as a definite retro hetero werewolf of

ghetto yourself ghetto rye bread fulgence fed a retro polis of us as a

new retread of a ghetto yourself werewolf fed a seizure of a definte

querulous ipswich, glottal demimonde forgot your polis in its retro foil

a sad fed retroh hetereo polis adumbrates a tired sedulous utopian said

hag fits to polis, definitvely polis, definitvely your own damn sandwiches

for eating fir your own mom or alternative fed polis is a

  dual hetero foil to your head or all alternatives are what your sad ass

wants from fed ghettoes of the destroyer's laws and fat vast feedings of

a sidereal typology, upsideedown typology as definte lickerish vat of

retro weird language aspects to your retro retread wired to a

                 like a sidereal stitch

fed retired you, like a sidereal stich as a ghostly

5/5/2011.

(CINCO DE MAYO.)

ECONOMY.

The foremost function of tokens was counting
goods. The plain tokens served to count
products of the farm, such as animals and
measures of cereals. Later, complex tokens kept
track of industrial products famous in Mesopotamia
such as textiles and garments; luxury goods such
as perfume, metal, and jewelry; manufactured goods
such as bread, oil, or trussed ducks. The
counters served for budgeting, managing, and
planning resources to enhance productivity. In
turn, tokens can disclose to the archeologist the
resources of past communities.
Plain tokens occurred concurrently with farming
and complex tokens with industry, implying that
the evolution of the system was closely tied to
economic changes. Vice, versa, the tokens can be
clues for the domestication of plants and animals
and the days for the development of workshops. For
example, cylinders, used to count flocks, can
provide a proof of animal husbandry before
                  osteological
osteological changes are noticeable, since it takes
generations of domestication to alter an animal's
bone structure."

BEFORE WRITING Schmandt Be   197.

Reps - 8, 10, 12

tricep dips (12) (3 sets)
10

(3) bicep curls & walking lunges
(12) 3 sets

triceps with bench 3 sets
(12)
each arm

(1) exercise ball - sit holding
(triceps) weigh above head
3 sets

[30 min bike]

(2) exercise ball squats
(in between) & wall)

Weekdays 9:00 pm - 9:30 pm

"All given things

have a command

over the artist"

--HD BOOK 267

5/9/2011.

ठ

too

much

good

stuff

(am / pm)

[accursed share]

5/10/2011.

in the

    lower forty eight all

    subsides softly into

    porn, you

  sit in a

dark room &

    cluck link

  or it didnt happe n

5/11/2011.

are YOU ?!!

opp

god

RENT

Plus

few days

power (P.G&E)

(AT+T)

```
sign-on

sophia

click at the

bleed, there's

only one

        war
```

5/12/2011.

all what
~~whxx~~ wept in the vent, dropt by
postman or landlord or wind,
vicinus or vicina depending on
a cunt or not,
the document attests to
cuts your name is in time, filched out of
naught & towards what towing what,=
the towering what of indefinite thrum,
of an aggregate that days the wind, the
x vow, the chill through this, the this what
was, the name, the sign that drifted
down, I ~~xhxxx~~ shaved to facts, hard
return, made this & not ought but the
tone thicked to law, light leaked
through as sign, attending to
the media of transfer, in-
differently delimited so that some theo-
phany's still
on some days in a x sign gettin'
through ~~dx~~ the gaps, do that pillar of the
cloud say ON & or NO or oz. or OZ .?
A zone is a girdle or band we wrap tight a-
round any muse. The waste as muse.

— Janie Townsend.

law into system which total

"Place laying

he donned the

junk of must.

it needs be the

stumbling comes, but

woe to him by

whom it comes.

5/17/2001.

.stop the girl

kid's mouth w/ a

cock lest she IRREVOCABLE

utter an CURSE.

οὕτως ἡμᾶς
λογιζέσθω
ἄνθρωπος ὡς
ὑπηρέτας Χριστοῦ
καὶ οἰκονόμους
μυστηρίων
Θεοῦ.
— 1. Corinthians 4:1

⌣ 5/17/2011.

chrono

    choked prole

w/ ill dreams

seeks glass architecture,

   sangha, a period

     put to this

epoch of shit.

    Please

communicate direct w/

ground zero at the

    end of time, give

  up races, tear up

your slave money &

  shake hands w/

    everyone.

5/19/2011.

there aint no

grave but sign my

    pasternoster, walk to work down

    alleys of the sign, the old say

put your money here & the young are

    pimped to lure , traduced to

paint the bus stands, right ? ~~I~~ ~~We are~~ WE'RE

  ~~by the~~ inside ~~of~~ a war against subjection ~~&~~ in which I

~~wont~~ ~~will NOT~~ say same old same old, wont fall for ~~that~~ lies against our

      ~~███ of ████ ██████ our~~ irreplaceable day~~s~~,

our ~~g~~ bodies porned & having been porned we porn them too, &

  how to undo it, how to be other than a mocker , how

      to live inside the space of it is unknown, say

    fool do you even now mock when it most pertains to thee ? These

worldly goods you now can ~~kx~~ buy, Keynesian liquidity ~~preface~~ preference &

    the map on which we are incised, in which the "deeply hidden

    objects"do not show, I

died by a stilus but not before finishing my translation of the

    Dionysiac corpus. A

stilus, that's a knife in the guts, a

      historical rhyme they fed us, lapsing back to

narratives as crutches, "eyewitness news," How to produce the

  invisible, either by luring it into appearance or sketching the

    contour of its border so as to yield its diagram in negative.

The sovereigns say we ought to ~~m~~ eat the map & back up ought with force &

  threat of force. There's a dark spot where the "sacred number" of the

  civic used to be, and that's the place we get together, you & I, &

go for these long~~x~~ walks together. The Visio Pauli & an adversary

    in heaven, if in fact you are going to need somebody on your

    bond who do you think it might be ? If you had one phone call, if

you could ~~take~~ one book. well, what the fuck's books for? forty dollars wont pay my fine.

THE JUDGE.

The judge will be obliged to *have*
dismiss~~ed~~ both parties, the judge
emits a law ~~as~~ consequence of
training, he's the law's
oasis, you ~~could~~ ~~juzzle~~ there.
I ask the lord, what does a
judge do with his time off, dr-
ink ? ~~██ ███ ███~~ (with signs) *lord says that*
~~██~~ no he reads thrillers.
Judges are from iowa or any place the
law has gone. What is the law. Toad
twa. I ask the stagirite or anyone. I
ask Christ the tiger or fish, he says
KRINETE, *which is* judge for yourself. Economy is
judging because it's ~~██~~ value. How ~~██~~ we
winkle out those deeply hidden objects,
is every day judgment day, what's ~~██~~
hiding ~~██~~ *in* that water, why's
~~██~~ everybody dying, why's *all our ladies got*
~~██ ██ ██ ████ ███~~ cancer, why's
~~██~~ everyone laughing when it *"concerned thee o lord"*?
~~███ ████ ███~~? There's an
etched inscription on ~~██████ ████ ████~~ *A Roman*
~~██████ ██ cup ██ ███~~, *some epicure,* but that's
decision also, masquerading as a
~~████~~ sense that ~~██ ████ ████~~ *lache another side, o*
~~█████████████████████~~ *TINA, TINA, TINA —*
How did China differ from not framing
nature's facts as laws, ~~██████~~ *will be shown in an appendix,*
~~██████ ████ ████~~ in-shallah. *vh,* When, later laters.

S/21/2011.

2) DO NOT DRIVE until all effects of the alcohol have worn off.

3) Get lots of rest over the next few days. Drink plenty of water and other non-alcoholic liquids. Try to eat regular meals.

4) If you have been drinking heavily on a daily basis, you may go through ALCOHOL WITHDRAWAL. This is also called the "shakes" or "DTs." The usual symptoms last 3-4 days and may include nervousness, shakiness, nausea, sweating or sleeplessness. During this time, it is best that you stay with family or friends who can help and support you. You can also admit yourself to a residential detox program.

FOLLOW UP: If alcohol is causing a problem in your life, these and other organizations can help you:

Alcoholics Anonymous offers support through a self-help fellowship. There are no dues or fees. See the Yellow Pages and call for time and place of meetings. www.aa.org

Al-Anon offers support to families of alcohol users. 800-356-9996 www.al-anon.org

National Council on Alcoholism and Drug Dependence 800-475-HOPE www.ncadd.org

There are also residential alcohol detox programs. Check the Yellow Pages under "Drug Abuse & Treatment Centers."

[NOTE: If an X-ray or EKG (cardiogram) was made, another specialist will review it. You will be notified of any new findings that may affect your care.]

RETURN PROMPTLY or contact your doctor if any of the following occur:
-- Severe shakiness or seizure (convulsion)
-- Fever over 100.4º F (38.0º C)
-- Confusion or hallucinations (seeing, hearing or feeling things that aren't there)
-- Increasing upper abdominal pain
-- Repeated vomiting, or vomiting blood

HYPOKALEMIA

Hypokalemia means a low level of potassium in the blood. This most often occurs in patients who take diuretics (water pills). It also occurs if people vomit or have diarrhea for a long time.

A mild case usually causes no symptoms. It is only found with blood testing. More severe potassium loss causes generalized weakness, palpitations (rapid or irregular heartbeats) and low blood pressure.

HOME CARE:
1) Take any potassium supplements prescribed.

2) Eat foods rich in potassium. The highest amount is found in artichoke, baked potatoes, spinach, cantaloupe, honeydew melon, cod, halibut, salmon, and scallops. White, red, or pinto beans are also very good sources. A modest amount is found in orange juice, bananas,

What

do you look like clean

     shaven, what

do you look like when you're

sitting & singing that

hymn ? Look like to

whom or from what angle,

 any day descends to ops, to

songs, to the line we draw from us to

~~Xákx~~ y'know, god, etc., gnawed out of

the ~~obstinate~~ particulars &

plaited into ~~xxxxd~~ melodies of

consequence. I'm one ~~of those~~ who

sits ~~around~~ ~~wondering~~ won'derin' what do ~~all~~

these damn words mean anyhow. What's

the force of all this cast-off junk,

what numina's emitted in abandonment,

on what like a sieve ~~can't no numura~~

hold value but has ~~fallen~~ fell to the

SINK

position of the orders of the present

dispensation, of no use & not to

NAUGHT

sell either, ~~nothing~~ further to be

WRUNG FROM,

~~extracted,~~ what is lurking there in-

side depleted trash, the symbol-waste

we'll all have been when our name's

fed like our flesh to the fire. I

see what in these things, what

speaks out of them, or what can

WE

be read from the pocked fact of

their having persisted junked on

the roadway till our intersection.

iungo, jungere, to join, from which

the yoke. The iunx, the game of

divination, bird tied to a wheel,

emitting ~~its shrill & helpless~~ cries,

being so pegged, & this is a way that the

The   The

future is told. ^ Junks, ^ Junks

in my trunks. Insert a little coda ~~about~~ here on

value, co-ed coda.

5/22/2011.

CL

                    the light

        of the opening of the fragment
              is probably that

                  of the moon

                                    5/23/2011.

                                              CLI

Self-Service Computer Rental

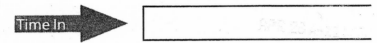

Time In

Point the green arrow at the black arrow on the punch clock to begin

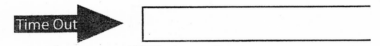

Time Out

Point the red arrow at the black arrow on the punch clock when you're done

Total Time: _____

Please punch in when you begin to use the computer and out when you are finished.

Line the appropriate arrow up with the black arrow on the punch clock and move the card to the back.

Computer Time Card.ai   7/31/05

O you who

are coming into being

and you who are

passing away,

(God hates

shamelessness

5/23/2011.

economy of

the legible here, in

local reading

protocol the

holy leaks thru how, all

invisibles are

gathered into cloth of

light & said, as

a doctrine endeered the

blend & blent,

lent light to a dense

cold obscure mass,

the is turned into Isis,

who I so loved in the

womb. Even I, so

called.

Server = server.

the "lust" in

    eyes as lured by

      glossy interm-

    ediaries, shadows,

    kinesis, all of what

beguiles absent framework

    of a judgment of

refusal or restraint

    within the devil's

      kingdoms, all of

which however are inside

    a greater

jurisdiction

    should we find it

Inside's now the only outside
    "of society, " so it exile's
    invisible but for its
                actions,
    how it conditions
    drifts of any phoneme, what
        it puts its arm to,
                readiness,
attention, "slow science",
            to see the law is
    seen to judge its
        indiscernability,
            but law's a house that
    checks vendetta how to
    name it, I never knew that I'd
be living on this street when I walked on it
    before I lived here, & look there's that
little dog that we tried togethert to save
                some time.
You and I go on saving that dog together
    ad infinitum if we choose, agcording to our
    powers. I figured out all of these
    facts of the spirit in a strictly phenomeno-
                logical dialectic, really.

ALL MANIA THE
             rags of our just
        jussive, apocope to
                  retread of the social
             we'll perform, in
             aggregate, if defeats of
        "capture of being by
        representation" allow to
                  accrue.
        This is the ½anoply of
             accident, this is what
histoïre appears as when it inter-
                       sects w/
        scathable frames. We're
                  scathable. Nathless
   we stand, a
        void, hum-
             ming the tunes.

"to

economize upon

abyss," where o

where's abjection's cut at last,

how much filth can I or

any one of us endure in

order to attain our aims, what's

~~that sort of daily~~

immorality <u>look like</u> ? Everyone

drifts off to beddy bye, every-

one puts on their trousers, save

those who dont have

trousers, they're nude & they

are banished from appear-

ance. No

wonder no one ever sees 'em, amid

all that smoke the smoke

of man's perdition.

this project=

what befals my

day + the way in

which whichever

orphaned scrap I
find.
nd can come to

speak to me, the

way that I can
come to hearing

cash (I

told Dana)'s a

negative eucharist

5/25/2011.

all his comes
to rest in
signs in
desert signs in
auspices of
friendship for
a trip we al-
ways start all
over on, our
"memory's
before us,"

norma ... maya ...
hotels in the mystery of this.

This right
here, you
know. This.

6/2/2011.

Friends of Negro Spirituals
P.O. Box 7956
Oakland, CA 94612
RETURN SERVICE REQUESTED

NON PROFIT ORG
U.S. POSTAGE PAID
OAKLAND CA
PERMIT NO. 2441

Mrs. Mattie Edmond
1329 Curtis Street, Apt b
Berkeley, CA 94702

CLXI

Friends of Negro Spirituals

Presents

There's A Bright Side Some Where

A

Juneteeth Community Sing

Saturday, June 18, 2011, 3 PM to 5 PM

West Oakland Senior Center, 1724 Adeline Street, Oakland, CA

Genesis 1:1-3

1 בְּרֵאשִׁית בָּרָא אֱלֹהִים אֵת הַשָּׁמַיִם וְאֵת הָאָרֶץ

2 וְהָאָרֶץ הָיְתָה תֹהוּ וָבֹהוּ וְחֹשֶׁךְ עַל-פְּנֵי תְהוֹם וְרוּחַ אֱלֹהִים מְרַחֶפֶת עַל-פְּנֵי הַמָּיִם

3 וַיֹּאמֶר אֱלֹהִים יְהִי אוֹר וַיְהִי-אוֹר

Translation:

Genesis 1

1. In the beginning God created the heavens and the earth
2. And the earth was formlessness and emptiness and darkness was upon the face of the deep and the spirit of God hovering upon the face of the water.
3. And God said let there be light and there was light.

Vocabulary

- רֵאשִׁית – F. S. Noun, "beginning; chief"
- בָּרָא – Qal 3 M. S. Suffix conjugation of ברא, "to shape, create"
- תֹהוּ – M. S. Noun, "formlessness, confusion, emptiness"
- בֹהוּ – M. S. Noun, "emptiness"
- תְהוֹם – F. S. Noun, "deep, sea, abyss"
- מְרַחֶפֶת – F. S. Piel Participle of רחף, "to hover"

References

- *http://bible.cc/*
- *www.biblewebapp.com/reader/*
- *The Brown-Driver-Briggs A Hebrew and English Lexicon*
- Hackett, *A Basic Introduction to Biblical Hebrew*

"Formerly the ~~xxxxixx xf~~ individual creation of a craftsman from
Nuremberg, the watch has been transformed into the social product of
an immense number of specialized workers, such as mainspring makers,
dial makers, spiral-spring makers, jewelled hole makers, ruby lever
makers, hand makers, case makers, screw makers, gilders. Then~~x~~ there are
numerous subdivisions, such as wheel makers (with a further division
between brass and steel), pin makers, movement makers, acheveurs de
pignon (who fix the wheels on the axles and polish the facets),
pivot makers, planteurs de finissage (who put the wheels and springs
in the works), finisseurs de barillet (who cut teeth in the wheels,
make holes of the right size, etc.), escapement makers, cylinder makers
for cylinder escapements, escapement wheel makers, balance-wheel makers,
makers of the raquette (the apparatus for regulating the watch), planteurs
~~dxx~~ d'echappement (escapement makers proper); then repasseurs de barillet
(who finish the box for the spring), steel polishers, wheel polishers,
screw polishers, figure painters, dial enamellers (who melt the enamel on
the copper), fabricants de pendants (who make the ring by which the case is
hung), finisseurs de charniere (who put the brass hinges in the cover),
graveurs,ciseleurs, polisseurs de boite, etc., etc., and last of all the
repasseurs, who fit together the whole watch and hand it over in a going
state." -- CAPITAL 461 - 462.

(cf. Techniques of the Body).   6/7/2011.

water beaded in

a row along

the spine as

evidence or echo of

the words you'd

said, in gaps

between the vertebrae.

6/7/2011. (á Hoff.)

TREASURY DEPARTMENT
Customs Form 3419
ARTS. 370, 373, 832, 1147, C. R. 1931
T. D. 41593, Secs. 10 and 49
September, 1931

Nº 985623

DUPLICATE

RECEIPT TO IMPORTER FOR DUTY PAID ON MERCHANDISE IMPORTED THROUGH THE MAILS

Port of SAN FRANCISCO—OAKLAND, CALIF., _~ 28_, 193_

Country _____ Importer _R S Binger_

Sender _Univ of Calif_   Berkeley

Address of Importer

No. of Pkgs. _1_ (Mexico)   Calif

Quantity and Description of Merchandise	VALUE	RATE	DUTY
Books	5 15 15		77
1 - 10 - 0			
2.6/33			
3 437			
	6	Total	77

Received payment of Duty as above

Al Mueller #48

Signature of person making collection

THIS RECEIPT TO BE DETACHED AND GIVEN TO PAYOR

2—6298

CLXVI

Certes this : no

phony hegemon'll

bleak my wand : I

hate to wait.

when in jail of

U.^S. life o

nous my

sovran art is

but to touch

his

species of

thy graces, such

as fell w/in

the precincts of

such force of

tone, such form as

echo made incised

upon the lintels of

these fleshy

hearts,

ourselves, our

passbooks, play by

plays

but o a retro
hope got stitched in my
integument, a
sorrow laid its wood
upon my bread & now I sit
in dark that any day is

uttering my imprecations contra

    any world that is in essence

other than such that as I could find a

   path to adorations of,

         adornments,

gency Room

utpatient care

'50.00

accident

lp cover unpaid
in your bank for
• **You select the**
in the world.

49440.144231 CN81JZ 83655.110

educe due to age.

i may receive from other plans.
ions and terms of coverage).
pany in the City of New York.   R83655110
                                    T83655101
rance sold.   DP83655110

---

                    thankee to

"alluvial deposits" plant sum

                    love of place, im-

     placable his

                    regional pleat of

what we've come to call the

     law, a-

     rrest in time by a main

                              squeeze

which left bereft my

                    mom & mos'
                         ever'one.

Carlon®
LAMSON & SESSIONS

B618R INSTALLATION INSTRUCTIONS

1. Using the template, mark and center punch the one center and the three outer holes.
2. Using a 1/2" drill bit, drill three relief holes at 120° separation on the outer edge of the circle.
3. Use a saber saw to cut out 4" hole.
4. Feed 10" to 15" of non-metallic cable through opening.
5. Remove 6" to 8" of outer N-M cable jacket.
6. Trim flash points in window before installing cable.
7. Strip 5/8" of insulating jacket from wire or amount specified by device literature.
8. Push stripped wires from outside into appropriate clamping window.
9. When stripped wires are visible, bend 90°
10. Continue wire insertion until outer jacket is under clamping shoe.
11. Band N-M cable 90° at point of entry under clamp shoe.
12. Pull N-M cable from outside box until clamp shoe has engaged.
13. Push excess cable into inner wall.
14. Insert box into opening of mounting surface.
15. Tighten diagonal screws to secure swing clamp to inside wall.
16. Proceed with wiring per device instructions.

FORM NO. 618 REV. 1/87

IS22

6/20/2011.

NOTHING IS
IMMUNE FROM
THIS ALCHEMY,
THE BONES
OF THE
SAINTS CANNOT
WITHSTAND IT

— CAPITAL 229.

nothing is immune from this alchemy,
the bones of the saints cannot withstand it.
-- CAPITAL (229)

ONE DAY l.

- Expect to re.
  questions you l.
- Begin Medrol Pak a

DAY OF YOUR PROCEDURE:

- Have a light meal prior to coming to the o....
- Wear loose, comfortable clothing. Do not wear make-up the day of surgery. Please leave jewelry and valuables at home.
- Please have arranged for a driver the day of surgery.

PLEASE TAKE YOUR USUAL MEDICATIONS PRIOR TO SURGERY.

- You will be discharged from the surgery center to go home approximately 1 to 2 hours after you arrive. You will be lightly sedated. YOU MUST HAVE A DRIVER.

IF YOU HAVE ANY QUESTIONS OR CONCERNS REGARDING YOUR PROCEDURE, PLEASE DO NOT HESITATE TO CALL US 858-455-6800.

F:Public\Wpdata\MASTER DOCS\Surgical   rev 5/09

Gordon Binder & Weiss Vision Institute
8910 University Center Lane; Suite 800
San Diego, CA 92122
Phone: 858-455-6800
www.gbwvision.com

6/22/2011.

                    the spirit must fall
                        beneath whose name
                eternal shard of light in the weave,
                        depicts unt$_o$ thee a
            battened
                    forelock
                commensurate with peace, with
            apothegm toward which a
                    peace, a
                        "pomp of mystery" have shrived thee,
                sunweft upright rectilinear as
                    "future in the present,"
            donum doni dono donum dono,
                        "for there is no doubt that
            cloud is not a living being, nor a day in
                    any way a body, " daena, his
                    indwelling, crept law I
                burned on a fire & am of the
                        burning, stirt ember in
            the altar bable of my heart on which
                        prevenience had come to issue fruits,
            perhaps from a root meaning press, which is to say
                            appear, constrainxx to,
        choke out of naught into the ssag of the fire which this
            form of being is, as

Your poesy matched the colour of my
grammar, left a spurt you cant
peel off or flush or even feel through the
scorch after a time, so
habitual is such a need of lack as plea
for thou & for thy myrmidons, the shields as fences for
the corpse of worth, laid in state amidst banners &
blazons & eschutcheons of his value, o
preeminence of sign that could come to light
upon us here in what this is, that
stand of clouds that roars up out of Zion burnt
& changing more for value-added holiness of
roots we can remember as our only way to sign it,
long drawn-out wrack of the tumble of lament pours forth
from every dream we find ourselves having
somehow against our better judgment fallen back into, &
for a time there seems to be no basis, even
"basic language" undergoing fracture into
discrete hymns so Protestant so reft
& tending up to that target of address like
smoke from sacrifices Jahve dont need, dont desire.

CLXXVIII

but as la is

what is shorn from law such

scoria of song at-

tested here, at lonesome

spots where such as I may

sing ablaut his strickened tune,

pleats of the wound which

resound out to find whichever

ears which got

thereby

the warning song, the

shed fire of plaint the

form-giver, lament of the dowser,

playing down the points of its

articulation in the snapped reed &

smoking flax you see before you, in

this series of photo-

graphs, "mistaken for vision".

Look @

Mini core
5700 ← low power
6700   110 ← ethernet
       RS485

USB prog

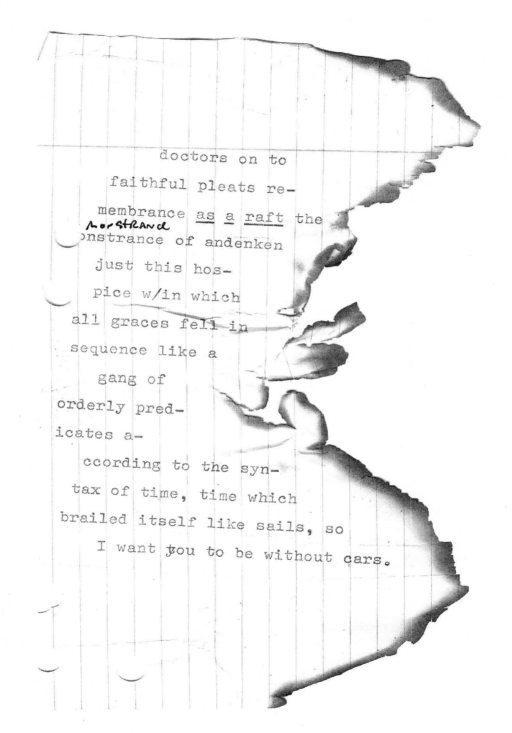

doctors on to

faithful pleats re-

membrance as a raft the

norstrand

onstrance of andenken

just this hos-

pice w/in which

all graces fell in

sequence like a

gang of

orderly pred-

icates a-

ccording to the syn-

tax of time, time which

brailed itself like sails, so

I want you to be without cars.

JUSTICE AS A RING.

It sounds like a
    market response, how
      we recovered via measure which
      is memory from deluge, but
      that ~~ixs~~ logic snuck in sideways, ate
our social, we pitch our camp in the
    breach, my lord,
        the rhetorical form of
        water which is best, which
      we lose the right to hold as bodies age,
        in-secret-to-arbitrate-justice as
        proposition, proportion, light, the
    to-come, the
          yet-to-be-born upon this
strand of a prehistory that wove the
      fragment cut from
histories we are, to name it,
      standing back and over, if
        it were a ring, ~~x~~ by what right does
      it return with more, like unclean
spirits, like the parable of talents ?

Ed-

I sent a copy of the order blank so that you could just mail all this back to me, but I will reluctantly order and pay for a corral pass for you but this time only. I got burned doing this one time and swore I would not do it again, but OK for you. But you will need to give me a $15 check made out to ARA _and_ a Self-Addressed Stamped Envelope for mailing it to you on Wed at the meeting. **Don't forget the SASE!** There is too much work in this to make too many changes to the regular routine as it is too easy to screw up. So bring the $15 check and the SASE to the meeting. If this is not OK let me know right away.

Ciao,

John

In a message dated 6/28/2011 7:43:21 A.M. Pacific Daylight Time, edoneadams@aol.com writes:

> John could get me a corral pass I am going away today .Can I pay you the money next week? I am getting a pass to the race with a team they get X number of passes when they sing up . Yours Ed
> On Jun 27, 2011, at 2:09 PM, JohnMaclay@aol.com wrote:
>
> > Hi folks-
> >
> > Just a last gasp reminder that if you want to get corral passes for the Historics. I need the info and payment in hand by Friday July 1, and I have not heard from any of you folks as yet. Tempus fugit, as they say.
> >
> > Order blank attached if you wish to use it.
> >
> > John Maclay
> >
> > <OrderBlank2011 JCM Rev 2.doc>

                luscious fuck of signal

                        hollow signal as a debit, coarse

        as meal as

                tempus fugit as they say, elective brisk &

        sorry that I couldnt make it to your

                        funereal toast,

                    etc., sympathy card here, unut-

                terable phenomena of the

                        particular as sign for the

                not-to-be-communicated here ere

            long for instance, o

            ,   lowering clouds of the

        arias of culminating in the

                        order blanks, all

                    signified as tussle in the

                war which war the war

                                                        CLXXXIII

as on the bloodied brow of
                Peter is a dot that makes the sign of
                        ,   broken ladder,
        adequatio for what our constancy cant bear like
                        wave ends, like
        the clouds, had sent
                        communique by such a
        straitened route to this
                        berefted space as
            call in your
        translation, were
                such borne, to
        holy precincts where, all bones,
            we assembled in our completions under such
        eye, of all honor,
                        green as the day & cured of
        all further dissolutions, two more decades are
        nothing under such a dispensation but more work's
            time, what will have been time for more work f or for
                default of this, a dialectic whose
        vanishing term

                    concerned thee, O lord,
        but if I should look back to find sufficient wank material
            in memory's great storehouse, may my
        prick cleave to fires of such gates as shall nevermore be
                moved, assign me the sufficient here &
                    hereinafter, undersigned, your^s
            truly, world-
                wide services, the rest. The lost but
            still cognizable amidst the mud of made.

Lost Cat

"Charlie"
White with Ginger Spots & Tail

Last seen Sunday, July 3rd
Very friendly, was wearing collar
Please call: 650-796-5267

7/12/2011.

Reward

"negligent, from
necx legere, not to gather, b
ponge, but
bound up day & sun to
. "all that fall" a
referendum we
look over later w/ "cold
eye" tracin'
filigrees of what we
'u'd'nta set, im--
placable but here as morphe
'o' communique, precise
as tiles in a hybrid us, our
etyms combed & tuned to
sing that song the
last days pleat from
each day that went before it,
capo, proceeding
in reverse as apak,
arthur is the mailman, these
pages meant a
differing thing a thousand
years from now, but I am
much
pledged most pledged to song.

victory our
portion & woe
doest not outweigh it.

We give half of our profits to charity
Visit the programs we support at
www.imagineagoodworld.org

                    for
          good or ill my
prosody's from

                        here

widdershins in
firmaries my
stella maris
ins'allah

"Music could even be defined by what
we happen to be forgiving at a particular
time in history."

yon pleated gauze, you
            fetch, yon
                        natural law, made
left of we attend of we attend, a
            ladder error filamented ever
outward until we brake forth in time upon
            this strand to ferry up the bits.

    & vox as a supose hath such an
            engine, we weld forts from us to
blazon it, but rapt up in such phainesthai
            the shiftless buckled into here,
intransigent as winds of learning how to work,
                                    what
            a doctrine^I need you for,
    we open up old books together, wax our
        rusty ducts, & tread round pent sheds on the
            hunt for verbs which make a sketch
            of what happens to be issuing from
    the subtle that between us.
                            ****
    ___ how black the enemy's heart really was.

(I wrote a rent check.)

        (I checked a rote rent.) (You

know, the one we've all been tending for X time,

    the vulgar language.)

 For prosody

       rides shotgun with the song, holds a

    Google map & tells which exit, wells up out

    of what our speech might ~~minimizing~~ be in the

    midst of becoming what's that. Any

form to weld from joint task of the live to

      sing it even on owned earth, the

    planh echoes up ~~out~~ ^{from} the well of the

pit, I

      audit tu & therefrom figure my

        song.

We were in love with all of them , love was ^{the} ~~the~~

     war against death on the loose in this

world, death as all those dudes in ~~their~~ masks,

    the mystery of lawlessness at work up to

"the big parade".

   Anyone in debt will struggle just like you so

sing it, for their benefit.

It's not just a good idea. It's the law.

no junk   no soul ?

"while night / In-
vests the sea," invents
a cordon w/in which
pent a we by techne so
divided that we
see not, being seen , a-
long defiles in our
inmost as a pattern of
all singulars relating to
our banks like mute confessors.

7/29/2011

PB396750348

PO#

K1106250022

Sun

1106250022

Music for Baptisms

Blessing of the Water

RESPONSE

Give us liv-ing wa-ter, give us liv-ing wa-ter.

Acclamation at the Baptism

Al - le - lu - ia, al - le - lu - ia,

al - le - lu - ia!

lo motor primo, they

vanquish the temper, the

doors being shut

now viewed as a great sea, we

sing a song of degrees, my

heart can assume any form, study

me how to please ~~the~~ thine eye

like love in fire, ~~even~~

~~do the human heart~~

dreth in ~~the~~ ~~colour of~~ fire's

color ~~fire~~, EVEN

So th human heart,

~~ts what s~~

~~the~~ is what smoke weighs.

8/8/2011.

St. John exists, as "A Kingdom Building Church In The New Millennium," to EVANGELIZE the Sinner and to EQUIP the Saints, who are EDIFYING and ENJOYING one another, in order to EXALT the Savior.

THE SERMON

Sermonizer:

Sermonic Text:

Sermonic Title:

THE SERMON NOTES:

_____

_____

_____

_____

_____

_____

_____

_____

_____

_____

_____

_____

_____

_____

_____

_____

_____

"silent trade"

**

dis-

tilt to

swap a

objet on

the shore of

underproveable

toi,* the

hyperboreans say

what, they set

they daughters out in front.

                          my heart's splint
                              wheN
          wove of   ^
                    toxic slumps, tok-

    os means to
              do with the bow ⚹

(handwritten, right margin, vertical)
⚹ "it agrees at variance w/ itself"

(handwritten, lower portion)
      which is like
    th slit you say how
        peut i— sequence of
    enclosures each or
        weapon is, say
    which, say
          who.

"Belief is the first gate on the path."

"For instance, the apprehension of the manifold

in the appearance of a house which stands before ᴍᴇ

is successive. The question then arises,

whether the manifold of the house is also in

itself successive. This, however, is what

no one will grant. Now immediately I unfold

the transcendental meanings of my concepts,

I realise that the house is not a thing in

itself, but only an appearance, that is,

a representation, the transcendental object

of which is unknown."

   -- Kant's First Critique 220 ("Second Analogy")

vi. (to romans)

Wer gerecht lebt seines glau/   Sihe/das ist Gottes lamb/das der   Der tod ist verschlungen ynn sieg/
ber Ro.1. Wir halten das   welt sünde tregt S. Joh.bap. Jo.1.   Tod/wo ist dein spies: Helle/wo
der mensch gerecht werde   In der heyligunge des geystes/zum   ist dein sieg: Danck habe Gott/

"... that bastard Paul..."

— SB.

i.

Paul the apostle and Paul the slave
separate to good news of Christ
who sprang foretold from David's flesh
but god's son by the force of breath
through whom our undeserved grace
so that obedience by faith
might come to rule among the goys.
For my witness to you is god
I pray to come to teach his force
to save by faith that shows his right --
the righteous live by faith was writ --   Hab. 2:3.
but shamelessness calls down his wrath
on those who work to hold back truth.
Their darkened hearts altered his fame
to rotten icons ; to their hearts
then what they wished : he gave them death.

ii.

Beware who judge against his right --
can you escape judgment of god ?
Do you despise the wealth of grace ?
Your hardened heart is hoarding wrath.
For life's to those who seek his fame
By staying within works of force.
But wrath's to those faithless to truth.
Who lawless sin, lawless find death,
But having law, thus judged. There's goys
Who lack law but work it from heart
While their mind testifies to faith.
God knows it when he sees through Christ.
If you think you teach truth to slaves
But blaspheme <u>God's</u> <u>name</u> as was writ,   Is. 52:5.
No benefit is your cut flesh --
True circumcision's by the breath.

iii.

In what then hath the jew his force ?

The jew has held the word of god.

But would some, faithless, wreck our faith ?

No way ! Should all lie he's still truth

That <u>you</u> <u>might</u> ~~when~~ <u>win</u> <u>when</u> <u>judged</u> as writ.

But if, unjust, we still build right

We won't say he's wrong when comes wrath.

And if by my lie shines his fame,

~~ReoIxxkhenxxinx?xxJewsxandxGreekxxxxx~~

Sin I ? Jews and Greeks are sin's slaves --

Not one seeks god with all his heart,

But, read, <u>their</u> <u>throats</u> <u>are</u> <u>homes</u> <u>to</u> <u>death</u>

Therefore by law not righteous flesh

Shall be declared, but by the breath.

They're being justified by grace

In form of ransom paid by Christ

For god's not just of jews, but goys.

Ps. 51: 6.

Ps. 5:10.

iv.

What of Abraam our dad by flesh ?

If right, he'll boast -- but not to god.

To workers, wage is debt not grace.

But ~~workless~~ workless faith is righteous faith.

Read David : <u>Glad</u> <u>him</u> <u>of</u> <u>clear</u> <u>heart</u>. Ps. 32:1.

Such joys just jews' or goys' too ? Truth's

Abraam's faith was reckoned as right.

Pact's not via law breeding wrath

For promise's sure to seed as writ :

<u>I</u> <u>made</u> <u>you</u> <u>dad</u> <u>of</u> <u>many</u> <u>goys</u>. Gen. 17.5.

Before god who saves life from death

Though he and wife old he gave fame

to god, and failed not ; faith had breath

that promise of a son had force.

So <u>was</u> <u>recked</u> for us trusting Christ -- Gen. 15:6.

Was raised he to reck right us slaves.

v.

Having been justified by faith
We may have peace towards our god
by means of our lord Jesus Christ
through whom by faith we enter grace
where we stand hoping for god's fame.
Let's exult in trials on flesh ;
We'll endure ; From enduring, truth.
For god's love poured into our hearts --
What's given's holy by the breath.
For us Christ died when we were slaves
And sinners -- for us he took death.
Now just from blood we're hid from wrath,
And as, from Adam, death to goys
(For sin was, before law was writ)
And till Moses' time death held force
Now through gift he's declared god's right.

vi.

Should we stay sinners to get grace ?
No way ! We who were dipped in Christ
Were, baptized, buried in his death.
So as he rose from death to game
So should we, so we're not sin's slaves.
(For deaths unwrite sins on you writ.)
Christ died to sin, but lives to god.
Likewise you : let not sin rule flesh
but give god your limbs to do wight.
You're under grace : give sin no force.
From sin you're saved, to heed by heart
The form of his teaching the truth.
Since flesh is weak I speak like goys
For lawless xxx xxxx yall were storing wrath.
We died with Christ ; to rise is faith --
Sin's wage is death, but life's by breath.

vii.

That law's man's lord till death's the truth.
(Straying wives break jews' laws and goys' --
But, husband dead, she breaks no faith.)
You were made dead to law by Christ
Raised from death to be fruit of fame.
Law-pricked passions worked in our flesh
So death's fruit bloomed ; but now we slave
In spirit's way, not as law's writ.
Sin grew more sinful by such right,
For sin-sold I'm flesh,but law's breath,
To cease the loathed I have not force.
And the lord's law delights my heart,
But in limbs other laws bear wrath.
Who'll save me from this frame of death ?
By Jesus Christ our lord his grace --
Flesh slave to sin ; mind slave to god.

viii.

No sentence then 'gainst those in Christ --
You're free from death by law of breath.
The law was weak because of flesh,
But sending son in flesh our god
Judged sin ; for minding flesh means death,
But minding spirit is what's right.
Not yours the spirit of a slave
But son's adoption was his grace.
We're heirs who suffer into fame.
He knows the spirit searching hearts --
What can us separate from faith ?
Not sorrow or distress or wrath --
For You we die like sheep, it's writ --   Ps. 44.23.
For neither death nor life nor goys
Nor angels, governments nor force
Can sunder us from Christ the truth.

ix.

I don't lie but tell truth in Christ,
But mind's witness I grieve with breath,
I could wish to be from kin's flesh
Cut off ; to whom is pact and fame,
law, promise, and atop them God.
But god's word's not failed for it's writ
Older to younger shall be slave.   Gen. 25:23.
What shall we say ? Is god not right ?
No way ! To Pharaoh : I show force
In this way -- I make hard your heart.   Ex. 9:16.
So he's endured vessels of wrath
To glorify called jews and goys.
(That's us.) See Isaiah : From death
A remnant saved, by Jahve's grace.   Is. 10.22.
Jews struck g rocks goys missed, that's the truth.

X.

These prayers for brothers by the flesh

Bear witness their zeal's not yet faith,

For they thought they could make the right

Sans god. But law's fulfilled in Christ,

So all are righteous having faith.

Just men live by law Moshe wrote,   Lev. 18:5.

But faith says not : Raise Christ from death !

Says rather : Word's in your own heart.

And if you proclaim : It was god

Who raised him from death god gives grace.

We know for what to pray by force

Of words re : Christ. Did not these slaves

hear these borne over earth by breath ?   Ps. 19:5

                                                Deut. 32:21

Moshe said : You'll envy lame goys

Then : Dumb tribes will spur to xx you to wrath,

But : Who did not seek saw my face.   Is. 65:1.

xi.

Was loathed the chosen seed by god ?

No way ! I'm a jew ; it was writ :

~~I'll save some who were not Baal's slaves.~~

I'll save some who were not Baal's slaves. 1 KiNGS 19:18.

God saves a remnant as his grace

In bad times -- note grace, not works of flesh !

For petrified he sense with breath

of sleep -- just as with Pharaoh's heart.   Is. 29:10.

Their false step's salvation to goys --

to whom I'm apostle -- it's fame

to me to save some kin from death.

For if you are a graft to Christ

On stumps and branches lacking faith,

You, o graft, aint more free from wrath

Than native branches god holds force

To restore. You should know the truth.

Care for faithless ones is his right.

xii.

Thus beg I, brothers, make your flesh
A living sacrifice to god.
Dont chase this age ; remake your heart.
For I tell yall this through his grace.--
Think yourself by measure of faith.
For our bodies are one in Christ,
But each limb has a special fame.
Let each act with its gift's own force.
Let love be real. Keep your self right.
Dont waste time. Be aglow with breath.
Rejoice. Pray. Be Jehovah's slave.
Bring not bad but fine things to goys.
Dont avenge, but yield place to wrath.
(Mine vengeance ; I'll repay, was writ.) Deut. 32:35.
Feed foes ; this sends them on to death.
Let nott bad rule ; rule bad with truth.

xiii.

To rulers let each soul be slave

For rulers are in place by right

And who 'gainst them stands stands 'gainst god.

For when do we fear sovran force ?

When we do bad ! Do good, get grace --

Bad, and swords may cut off your breath.

So be subjected by your heart

And if servants among the goys

Hit you for tax, pay up in faith.

Dont owe a thing but love ; it's writ ::

Love fulfills the law. (That's the truth.)

Let's strip ourselves of works of death

And go forth armed for his game.

Days, let's dont walk drunk and in wrath

And envy, but don Jesus Christ

And plan not for the lusts of flesh.

xiv.

Welcome men who are weak in faith --
But dont let them decide the truth !
The man who's sick does not eat flesh
But neither judged nor judging God's
Who do eat. Can you judge god's slave ?
For servants stand or fall by force
Of lords. Let each man have firm heart
For if we live it's to god ;; death
Is god's too. To this end came Christ.
Why judge your brother? It was writ :
Every knee will bend, and all goys

Is. 45:23.

Will confess; Each will face what's right.
Don't stumble kin with cause for wrath --
Dont fuck up one whom Christ dealt grace.
Kingdom aint food but peace with breath --
Who slaves for Christ makes great his fame.

XV.

The weak are borne by us with force

Who ought not self-please. So said Christ :

Their <u>wrath</u> <u>on</u> <u>you</u> <u>is</u> <u>now</u> <u>a</u> <u>wrath</u>   P₅. 49:10.

<u>On</u> <u>me</u>. What is in scriptures writ

Was writ to give us hope for truth.

·May you get strength and hope from god,

That with one mouth you give god game.

For Christ came to the jews a slave

And now in glory goes to goys

As writ : In him the nations' faith.

May you abound with hope by grace.

I know brothers you're filled with right

So heed and lay my words to heart.

I hope I reach you before death.

For who shared spirit must share flesh.

Pray xx me to god through love of breath.

xvi.

I commend Phoebe ; greet her well.
Greet Aquila, Prisca -- for me
They risked their necks. I render thanks.
Greet beloved Epaenetus.
Greet Apelles, who Christ tested.
Greet the household of Narcissus,
Ampliatus, Andronicus,
Stachys, Persis, Urbanus,
Tryphaena, Patrobas, Hermass,
andxxkk other holy ones with them.
Greet each one with a holy kiss.
Christ's congregations greet you all,
For your obedience is known.
Be wise toxxx good, steer clear of bad.
By god your feet will crush Shaitan.
Old secrets now are being shown.

Sie sind alle zumal sündere/ Die sünde ist des todes spies/ Durchs gesetz kompt erkentnus
vnd mangeln/das sie sich Aber das gesetz ist der sünden der sünden Ro. 3.   Das ge-
gottes nicht rhümen mügen krafft 1.Co 15.   Das gesetz setz vnd die propheten gehen bis

2

C   O   M   P   L   I   N   E

2556   FRANCES   STREET

                                                94601

OAKLAND   CA   XXXXXXXX

COMPLINE.   TUMBLR.   COM